ESSAYS NEAR AND FAR:

As a New Century Dawns

By Robert V. Keeley

Five and Ten Press Inc.
Washington D.C.
2002

This is a Black Sheep Book
published by Five and Ten Press Inc.
Black Sheep Books are sold by subscription
as well as individually.
See pages 117 to 124 if you would like to buy a copy
of this book or any of our other publications.

First Edition
This is a limited edition of 400 copies; 300 have been
numbered and signed by the author for our subscribers.

Number _288_

Robert V. Keeley

Printed in the United States of America by Thomson-
Shore, Inc.

Library of Congress Control Number: 2002103468

ISBN 1-892379-17-1

CONTENTS

This collection is dedicated to

Nelson Mandela

a minor terrorist and one of history's
greatest freedom fighters.

By a fortuitous coincidence the young lady working
at the Middle East Policy Council who faxed me my essay
entitled "Trying to Define Terrorism" for checking and
proofreading also faxed me by accident the text of an
essay by Mandela destined to be published in the same
issue of *Middle East Policy*. Mandela's was entitled "A
Global Partnership in the Quest for Peace." Not only is it
a great honor to be included in the same publication as
Mandela, but his is a masterful appeal for international
cooperation that merits wide readership. His essay was
actually the fourth in an annual series of "Sadat Lectures,"
delivered on November 14, 2001, at the University of
Maryland, just two weeks before my talk on terrorism at
the Center for International Policy included herein.

There is one error in Mandela's lecture--one made
often, it must be said--about who attacked whom first in
the Arab-Israeli war of 1967. One error per essay is
tolerable, I believe, and I hope that my own efforts that
follow will not exceed that standard.

This book has been edited, as usual,
by my daughter, Michal Keeley.

CIVILITY IN DIPLOMACY

Today, as we all know, is March 20. I have a book that I consult whenever I give a talk that among other things contains a catalogue of famous events in American history listed by the date on which they occurred. Here's the entry for March 20, citing an event that happened way back in 1852. It was the publication date of the famous book by Harriet Beecher Stowe entitled *Uncle Tom's Cabin*. As you all know, that book, and a later stage production based on it, played a major role in the anti-slavery movement of the time. Well, was that the most noteworthy event of March 20 in our history? Here's what one authority, Abraham Lincoln, said when he first met Mrs. Stowe: "So you're the little woman who wrote the book that made this great war!"

What does that have to do with civility, or with diplomacy? I'll get to that in a few minutes, but just keep in mind that a book apparently started a war.

The person who asked me to take on this speaking assignment made it clear that this was to be an after-dinner talk, after a long half-day of intense intellectual engagement, and I should therefore be careful not to be too heavy or demanding, that I should keep it light and relaxed, as he put it. So before getting into the subject of civility in diplomacy, I thought I'd recount to you the last time I took on such an assignment with those rules of engagement. This tale could be called an illustration of stupidity in diplomacy, not civility.

This was the after-dinner address at the Cosmos Club's symposium on "Civility" in Washington, D.C., delivered on March 20, 1999.

In the early 1980s I was serving as the first American ambassador to the new country of Zimbabwe in southern Africa, the former Southern Rhodesia. One of the principal tasks I undertook, voluntarily and because I believed in its importance--it was also official if unstated U.S. policy--was to try to help convince the white community of Zimbabwe to remain in the country and help the new experiment in a black-majority-ruled former crown colony and recent breakaway independent country that had just barely survived a bitter race-based civil war and international sanctions regime. The purpose of keeping the whites in the country and engaged was to better the odds of the Zimbabwe experiment succeeding, and if possible to set an example for South Africa, a much graver problem in which the entrenched white minority was still fiercely resisting the idea of eventual black majority rule.

So I accepted any and every invitation to speak to a white audience, and did so on probably 40 to 50 occasions during my tour in that country. Though I of course tailored my remarks to the audiences in question, most of which were members of various white commercial farmers groups, a key element for economic stability and progress, the pitch I gave was generally one of encouragement to give Zimbabwe a fighting chance and to stick it out despite the ups and downs in morale that they were sure to experience.

One year as the Christmas season approached I received an unusual invitation to address a group in Bulawayo, Zimbabwe's second city and the capital of Matabeleland province in the southwest. It came from the president of the Matabeleland Society of Chartered Accountants, who held a black tie annual dinner on New Year's Eve for their members, their spouses and guests. The president asked me, given the holiday spirit of the occasion, to make a light and relaxed presentation, with some humor and cheerfulness. This admonition caused me to scrap my usual pitch, which the audience would no doubt deem heavy in the extreme. I thought I could introduce my appeal subtly in a question-and-answer period to follow my talk. So I prepared an entirely fresh talk that I thought would serve to amuse this audience of accountants.

I didn't know much about accountants then, and what transpired was a decidedly educational experience. I wouldn't want to say that the chartered accountants of Matabeleland were a humorless bunch, that is, an entirely humorless bunch, but I clearly made a very bad calculation as to what they might find amusing. The title and theme of my talk was "Why Everybody Loves Inflation." I have long been an amateur economist, with the emphasis on amateur (as I have no credentials in that field whatsoever), and occasionally a supposedly bright idea will strike me that runs completely contrary to conventional economic theory and practice. I should note that I gave this talk at a time when we were experiencing double-digit inflation in the United States.

Warming to my theme, I said that the smartest thing a young person could do would be to take out the largest 30-year home mortgage for which he could afford the monthly payments, because 20 or 25 or 30 years down the road those payments would have become a very small fraction of his monthly income, and the repayments of principal--most occurring in the late years of the mortgage--would be in greatly debased dollars compared with the dollars he had borrowed years earlier to buy the house. All of this due to inflation.

Who else likes inflation? Life insurance companies. They sell you a policy when you're young, you pay the premiums in today's and tomorrow's dollars, and when they pay your heirs the death benefit many, many years later, it's in debased currency, in dollars that have lost much of their value during your lifetime owing to inflation. During all that time the insurance company was investing your premiums and taking a cut for itself. Even casualty companies benefit. You pay the premium at the beginning of the policy year, the company uses that money--it's called the "float"--to earn money for itself by investing it, while the payouts to any policyholders making claims occur throughout the year. If you try to pay the premium in installments, they hike the premium.

Trade union leaders like inflation. They can keep claiming wage increases because of inflation, whereas if there was no inflation, no one would ever get a wage increase and workers would be extremely unhappy with their stagnant wages. They would blame their leaders. It's ingrained in our culture that everyone likes to think he's better off this year than last year. An increase in earnings, even if it's eaten up by inflation, makes people think they are doing better. It's an illusion, but a pleasant one.

Politicians like inflation. It constantly increases revenues, so that governments can vote bigger appropriations for popular programs, and no one's the wiser that there's been no real increase at all. Inflation helps folks get reelected. Pensioners whose pensions are automatically indexed for inflation aren't bothered by inflation, and that includes Social Security recipients. In fact they make a gain, because with the exception of increased medical expenses, pensioners don't consume a lot of the stuff that goes into the consumer price index that is the basis for raising their pensions. Things that are already paid for or no longer needed, like housing, transportation to work, office apparel, education, meals downtown. And for most pensioners Medicare takes care of a lot of the medical expenses. Anyone who buys now

4

and pays later likes inflation, especially if he can pay a lot later. Every time I buy a suit, the salesman talks me into buying two because, he says, the price is going up next year. He's right. But I'm stupid.

Are there any people who dislike inflation? Yes, there are. People who already have lots of money. Inflation reduces the value of their cash. Of course inflation will push up the rates of interest they can earn from lending their money or investing their capital, but when they get that capital back it's not worth as much as it was before. The nominal value of their assets will rise, but there may be a lag before they catch up. Someone who has no savings at all is not hurt by inflation because he spends all of his cash as fast as it comes in.

To that point in my talk the expressions on the faces of the chartered accountants in the audience varied from a quizzical frown, which I interpreted to mean that these people were wondering whether I was serious or was trying to be funny, to glazed-over eyes, from either too much wine or a total lack of interest in the subject of inflation, to some people who were already sound asleep. I then moved on to my principal point, which I hoped would wake them all up. And arouse them it did.

I had long wondered at the curious phenomenon that annual reports of corporations and other business entities, designed to impress their shareholders, customers, regulators, and anyone else interested, never report their performance in constant dollars--or whatever other currency they work in. Zimbabwe, by the way, uses the dollar, the Zimbabwe dollar. What struck me was that no business report ever took account of inflation. Thus if inflation in a given country was on the order of say 5 percent, and the annual report presented an overall picture of 10 percent growth in sales, 10 percent growth in revenues, 10 percent growth in profits, 10 percent growth in dividends, 10 percent growth in stockholders' equity, and 10 percent growth in the stock price, those figures were 100 percent deceptive, for half of the growth in each one of those figures was the result of inflation and in no way accounted for any amount of genuine growth. The figures used in the report were exactly double what they should have been, if one wished to be honest and use constant dollars.

The question I posed for the accountants in Bulawayo was why they went along with such deceptions, since I believed their professional responsibility was to present a true picture of the performance of the businesses for which they did accounting and auditing. Of course the phony growth figures would keep the unobservant stockholders happy, and would win thankful approval for the company's executives and most likely some performance bonuses, and since everyone did it, no one, not even government regulators or stock exchange officials, would think to criticize.

To drive the point home I had prepared some large visual aids, some colorful charts on big cardboard sheets that I displayed on an easel, a set of bar charts that the producers of annual reports are so fond of using, with the results displayed to show year-on-year progress marching ever upward, as for example in this chart (Figure 1). It shows 10 percent annual growth rates over the past five years. Very impressive, except that these bars happen to include 5 percent inflation. Here is a second chart (Figure 2), which shows the same data as the first chart but which cuts out the bottom half of the scale on the left in order to make the annual rise in performance even more dramatic. This is a technique I learned from reading one of my favorite books, *How to Lie with Statistics*.

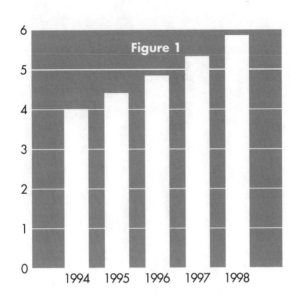

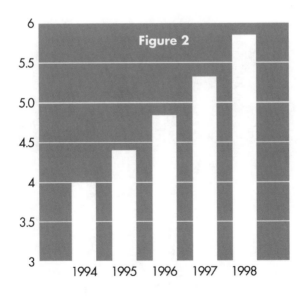

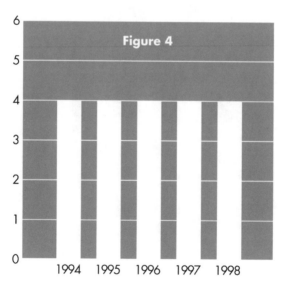

8

Then I showed the Bulawayo accountants a third chart, like this one (Figure 3), with the bars expressed in constant dollars, eliminating the contribution of inflation, and no trickery by leaving out the bottom half of the scale. Not quite as impressive, is it? This one is of course much less flattering to the company and its executives. All three of those charts use the very same data, the same actual performance. Even less flattering is this fourth visual aid (Figure 4), which shows the results of a company with annual growth rates in all the relevant areas of 5 percent, which in an environment of 5 percent inflation shows no growth at all, when the data is expressed as it should be in constant dollars. The company is going sideways, and most likely everyone responsible will be fired, that is, if anyone ever sees a chart like this one.

Needless to say, the Matabeleland accountants were stunned by this presentation at their festive New Year's Eve banquet. Not only were they not amused--there was not a single laugh or guffaw during my entire talk--and as I finished they mostly sat on their hands and held their mouths in a grim or pouting expression. They displayed an absence of civility in their reaction to my talk, and no doubt they thought I had been extremely uncivil in bringing up such unpleasant material in a talk at their annual banquet. Regardless of how they personally and individually felt about staying on in Zimbabwe, they were probably unanimous in feeling that the sooner I left the country the better all around. Needless to say, there was only perfunctory applause, and no question-and-answer period followed, as everyone wanted to change the subject.

All of what I was saying then is still true today, even though we are now in a period of low inflation. This idea was not original with me. A word about Berkshire

Hathaway, a company with a net worth (not market capitalization) of 58 billion dollars, the highest of any company in the U.S. Berkshire is the holding company of Warren Buffett, who owns about 40 percent of the company and manages it by himself while paying himself a salary of only 100,000 dollars a year. At this time of year every year, those of us who have invested in Berkshire look forward to receiving Buffett's annual report, for he is America's most successful investor. Every year his report is filled with gems of Buffett's wisdom about the economy, business, and investing.

This year he dropped a bombshell. As reported last Monday by *The New York Times*, he leveled "an extraordinary attack on many of his fellow chief executives, who he says have worked purposefully 'at manipulating numbers and deceiving investors' through accounting gimmicks and misrepresentations. 'Many major corporations [Mr. Buffett wrote] still play things straight, but a significant and growing number of otherwise high-grade managers--C.E.O.'s you would be happy to have as spouses for your children or as trustees under your will-- have come to the view that it's O.K. to manipulate earnings to satisfy what they believe are Wall Street's desires.'" Buffett continued: "These managers ... also argue that in using accounting shenanigans to get the figures they want, they are only doing what everybody else does. Once such an everybody's-doing-it attitude takes hold, ethical misgivings vanish."[1]

Three days before this news report Berkshire stock had made a spectacular 6.5 percent jump of 4,900 dollars to a high of 80,300 dollars per share. To account for this

---

[1] *The New York Times*, March 15, 1999, pages C1, C2. This was two years and nine months *before* the Enron scandal broke.

sudden rise there must have been some illicit "insider" knowledge of what was in Buffett's annual report other than criticism of his fellow corporate executives. The annual report was posted on Berkshire's Web site over last weekend. And Wall Street then had its revenge. On Monday, the day that the *Times* reported Buffett's assault, the stock fell back 5.8 percent to where it was before, and the next day it fell another 4.3 percent, as the overall market was setting new records. Later in the week Berkshire bounced back up, as it always does. Buffett never loses--in the long run.

I wouldn't be surprised if my personal stock, that is, my reputation, takes a plunge after tonight.

I could have used the title: "Why only Alan Greenspan hates inflation." I believe he genuinely does dislike inflation. After all, part of his job is to protect the assets of the people who have lots of cash, and as I mentioned earlier, such people can be hurt by inflation. But in testimony before Congress not very long ago, the day after the president's "State of the Union" address, Mr. Greenspan avoided saying two crucial things that he knows very well are true:

Number One--That there is no budget surplus, not now, not in the coming year, and there's no guarantee there ever will be a genuine surplus. Ever since the administration of President Lyndon Johnson we have had a so-called unified budget, that is, one that includes Social Security receipts and outlays. For many years the receipts have exceeded the outlays, so there has been a budget surplus in that part of the budget, disguising the deficits in the rest of the budget. This was originally done at the behest of a bipartisan commission, but its real purpose was to disguise the cost of the Vietnam War and to deceive our people into believing that we could have both guns and butter with no pain for anyone.

Number Two--Mr. Greenspan did not dispute the totally erroneous canard that recipients of Social Security benefits receive much more than they ever paid in in taxes. That is false. The payroll taxes that workers and their employers paid into the Social Security Trust Fund over a working life of 40 to 45 years were paid in dollars that had a much higher value than the current benefits they receive in today's dollars that owing to inflation have been debased over the many years they were working. Also, one must take into account as a cost or contribution the interest that those payroll taxes could have earned had they been invested for the benefit of the Social Security recipient in retirement.

Yes, I realize I was supposed to be speaking about civility. Actually, that is what I have been doing, because I found that there was a gap in our program today, to wit, civility in economics, and to a greater extent in politics. Economics is an area of modern intellectual discourse that is often lacking in civility because economics tries to be a science, if a dismal one, when it should actually be part of the humanities, because economics has enormous effects on the welfare of human beings.

I believe I've just provided evidence that since my retirement from the Foreign Service I've become much more interested in economics than in diplomacy. That may be true and natural for anyone moving from a salary to a pension. By this time in the evening you must be wondering if I didn't understand the topic I was assigned to talk about, or that I have been deliberately avoiding that subject, "Civility in Diplomacy." The latter is partly true, and the reason is that I have so little to say on that subject. And the reason for that is that in essence civility *is* diplomacy and diplomacy *is* civility when contrasted with what their opposites may be, with what their alternatives are.

Civility is diplomacy, or diplomacy is civility, in the sense that diplomacy is designed to prevent or ameliorate conflict, in its most important aspect to prevent war, whether hot war, cold war, trade war, propaganda war (that is, a war of words), civil war (an interesting term for an extreme absence of civility, for civil war is in many ways the worst kind of war, with the greatest brutality), or any other form of war. In essence diplomacy and civility are synonymous or interchangeable. Therefore there is not much original to be said about them.

I would amend Karl von Clausewitz's famous dictum that "war is merely the continuation of policy by other means" by substituting the word "diplomacy" for the word "policy" and by reversing the phrase to say that diplomacy is a substitute for war by using other means. I much prefer the very simple formulation attributed to Winston Churchill, who said: "To jaw-jaw is always better than to war-war." Another formulation I like is by Montesquieu: "Nations ought in time of peace to do to one another all the good they can, and in time of war as little harm as possible, without prejudicing their real interests."

In diplomacy there are obviously various kinds of civility. So I've looked back a bit into our diplomatic history as well as at the contemporary scene and have come up with a catalogue, a short list, of 22 kinds of civility in diplomacy. We can even include some examples associated with members of the Cosmos Club--deceased members, I should add.

Gunboat Civility: In the 19th century it was common for one of the major powers, if it had a navy, and they all did, to send a diplomatic message by sailing a gunboat into the principal harbor of a minor power, the ship's guns at the ready, and to have the captain or admiral deliver an oral or written message that that minor power should cease and desist doing whatever it was that was annoying the major power. This kind of tactic no longer seems feasible, and it has been replaced by somewhat subtler but no more effective means of communication.

Big-stick Civility: In 1900 President Theodore Roosevelt stated: "I have always been fond of the West African proverb: 'Speak softly and carry a big stick, you will go far.'" This gave a name to a central principle of his foreign policy of justifying American intervention in the Caribbean and Latin America. The doctrinal basis came to be known as the "Roosevelt Corollary" to the Monroe Doctrine, the latter having been originally designed to prevent European intervention in the Western Hemisphere. In his 1904 annual message to Congress, Roosevelt's "Corollary" stated that "Chronic wrongdoing ... may in America, as elsewhere, ultimately require intervention by some civilized nation, and in the Western Hemisphere the adherence of the United States to the Monroe Doctrine may force the United States, however reluctantly, in flagrant cases of such wrongdoing or impotence, to the exercise of an international police power."

Dollar Civility: The term "dollar diplomacy" is associated with the administration of President William Howard Taft and his secretary of state, Philander P. Knox. This approach supplanted or extended the big-stick policy. It was aimed at Central America and it had a dual character. On the one hand it was the use of diplomacy to advance and protect American business interests abroad, and on the other hand it was the use of American dollars abroad to promote the ends of American diplomacy. The Monroe Doctrine was again the justification. At various times it was directed against Nicaragua, Honduras, Guatemala, Haiti, and the

Dominican Republic, and the instruments used included open interventions, ousting dictators, putting down rebellions, landing Marines, taking over the countries' customs through receiverships to pay off their debts, arranging bank loans, promoting democracy, and generally restoring order. President Woodrow Wilson placed the emphasis on promoting democracy, and declared: "I am going to teach the South American republics to elect good men!" President Franklin Roosevelt changed all that and formalized a Good Neighbor Policy in the 1930s, although the term "Good Neighbor" was actually invented by his predecessor, Herbert Hoover.

Successful Civility: I suppose the best recent example of this is the Good Friday agreement to settle the conflict in Northern Ireland. Former Senator George Mitchell didn't win the Nobel Peace Prize, but as the mediator he probably deserves more credit for the outcome than he has received.

Failed Civility: The best recent example I can think of is the failure of the Oslo Accords between Israel and the Palestinians to produce a Middle East comprehensive peace. That agreement seemed like a breakthrough at the time, but the peace process has bogged down, though I certainly hope that's not the end of the story.

Excessive Civility: Another word for this is appeasement. The best historical example is still Munich, and the appeasement of Nazi Germany and the fueling of Hitler's appetite by sacrificing the small, weak power of Czechoslovakia. The sellout will always be associated with the figure of Neville Chamberlain and his statement that he had achieved "peace in our time."

Lying Civility: There is no better example than what Hitler said at Munich: That the Sudetenland "is the last territorial claim which I have to make in Europe."

Illegal Civility: This refers to the Iran-Contra scandal. The motive was not a bad one. It was to free our hostages being held in Lebanon. There being no possibility of a successful military operation to free them, a kind of diplomacy was tried. But it completely violated our long-standing policy of not paying ransom for hostages, and this case was even worse in that it involved delivery of arms as ransom, and to an unfriendly state. And then the violation was compounded by using the proceeds of arms sales to Iran to finance the Contras in Nicaragua, in direct defiance and contravention of the expressed will of Congress. Civility that is illegal is not civility.

Duplicitous Civility: I don't have a really good example of this, for all diplomacy is somewhat duplicitous. If we told the unvarnished truth to our diplomatic interlocutors, we'd probably be insulting them, and that would limit our effectiveness severely.

Indifferent Civility: The refusal of the European powers to deal with the issue of the breakup of Yugoslavia and the bloodshed and ethnic cleansing in Bosnia, in the early stages when foreign intervention might have been successful. The Europeans were being civil in staying out of the conflict, but uncivil in ignoring the suffering.

Delayed Civility: Bosnia again, but this time our own reluctance to get involved. We thought the Europeans would or should take care of this problem, but they didn't. Germany was partial to the Croats; Russia, France, and Greece were partial to the Serbs; only Turkey (among NATO powers) was partial to the Bosnians, but it had to stay out, as the Bosnian Muslims were a leftover from the years of the Ottoman occupation. Who helped the Bosnians? Iran, a rogue state from our point of view. We dithered while the atrocities and systematic ethnic cleansing horrified the world. This was a place for diplomacy and civility, but by the time we stepped in the situation was beyond repair, and about all we could do was impose a truce and thereby ratify the new borders that had been created as a new and recognized status quo.

Imposed Civility: This is what Richard Holbrooke did at Dayton, Ohio, when he forced the contending parties in and around Bosnia to agree to a settlement that none of them actually wanted, and that they are sure to subvert, sabotage, and overturn when they get a chance. Nevertheless it was a major achievement in that it stopped the bloodshed, at least for some time. That was about all that could be achieved, at least at that time.

Misguided Civility: Our negotiating with Slobodan Milosevic because he's the head of state or government who we think can influence events. He sure can, but he's a war criminal and should be tried as such, not negotiated with. He's responsible for the atrocities in Kosovo (which all started with his taking away the autonomy of the province), following on his launching of the Bosnian war and ethnic cleansing.

Desperate Civility: The granting of amnesty to the surviving leaders of the Khmer Rouge. They should also be tried as war criminals, but the situation of Cambodia is so desperate that the government there believes it has to grant amnesty to start the country on the road back to health. I have mixed feelings about this, but I think trial by an international tribunal would be a mistake, and would be an intrusion by outsiders into a very difficult domestic situation that the Cambodians should be allowed to handle by themselves without outside interference. In the case of crimes of genocide or other atrocities committed as part of a civil war, not an international war, once peace has been reestablished, I think the nation itself should be the authority to deal with the problem. As imperfect as the process has been, I think the example of South Africa with its post-apartheid Truth and Reconciliation Commission has been a good example of how to proceed.

Revisionist Civility: I refer here to the 1,151 pages of the third volume of the diplomatic memoir of Henry Kissinger. A review published in *The New York Times* on March 17 by Richard Bernstein contained the following paragraph: "Mr. Kissinger uses his 3,800 pages [of the complete memoir] to make his case against his critics and detractors, trying, as he works through the years, to demolish the various 'myths' that, in his view, have accumulated around him (among the more important of them is that he did not attempt to negotiate a solution to the war in Cambodia and is indirectly responsible for the triumph and the atrocities of the Khmer Rouge)." So two days ago I shelled out 35 dollars for the book, *Years of Renewal*, and I read the chapter about the fall of Cambodia. All I'm prepared to say at this time is that this instance of revisionism will require some revision.

Lecturing Civility: This is what has been going on recently in our bilateral relations with China. We have been lecturing China about its very poor human rights performance, and complaining about its sales of weapons and technology to other countries that we don't like or that at least we don't think ought to have those things that China is selling to them, and being upset about alleged Chinese spying on us and theft of some of our important nuclear weapons secrets. At the same time China is lecturing us about our support for Taiwan, particularly in the military sphere, and we find this objectionable, just as it considers our human rights lectures to be interference in its internal affairs.

All the time we are madly trading with each other,

for that is what both of us are really most interested in. We are a great market for Chinese exports, and the vast Chinese population has our exporters drooling over the prospects of selling American stuff to all of them. By the way, we claim to be worried about the negative balance in our trade with China; currently they sell us a lot more than we sell to them. But were you aware that about 60 percent of what China sells to us are the products of American firms manufacturing in China? Who do you think is making money from this trade imbalance?

And on Taiwan, now we are proposing to build a so-called theater missile defense system to protect Japan, South Korea, and Taiwan. The first two are OK, but how do you think the Chinese feel about our establishing a protective ring around what they consider a renegade province of their own territory, to protect it from the motherland? No wonder China has planted a whole bunch of missiles on its coast opposite Taiwan. In similar circumstances wouldn't we do the same? Which brings me to:

Missile Civility: Speaking of missiles, some folks in positions of power in this country are determined that we spend tens of billions of dollars to create an anti-missile defense. This is a ridiculous expenditure and a violation of our long-standing nuclear policies that prevented a nuclear disaster when we and the Soviets were engaged in MAD--mutual assured destruction. If some rogue enemy state--North Korea, Iraq, Iran, Libya, you name it-- were able to build a missile to reach our shores and were so insane as to actually launch one or more our way, that would be detected immediately and we would know the origin, and that origin would soon be obliterated in retaliation. Therefore no such state, unless its leaders were totally suicidal, would ever launch a nuclear missile. That is what kept the nuclear peace with the Soviet

19

Union, in the age of nuclear deterrence and the balance of terror. What we have to fear today is something quite different.

Today Russia has about 200 tons of plutonium, the basic ingredient needed to make a bomb. Most of that plutonium is under uncertain military control that we hope and pray will be effective. But some 20 tons or more is in the Russian energy sector, not under the same kind of control, and perhaps available for clandestine diversion to bad guys, terrorists or others who wish us harm. All they need to do is make a bomb--the technology is well-known, having been published in *Popular Mechanics* by a graduate student, among other places--using about five kilograms of plutonium (that's 11 pounds) that can be carried into this country in a small suitcase by a passenger on a ship, and then detonated to destroy a major city. To keep you from being frightened, let's call that city Baltimore and not Washington. The identity of the perpetrator will never be known, so there is no possibility of retaliation and therefore no deterrent threat of retaliation, and thus no way to prevent it. That is what should be giving us nightmares. A nationwide missile defense system will do nothing to prevent that. What it really is is corporate welfare for our defense industries and their associated contractors, at taxpayer expense.

Alliance Civility: Next month here in Washington we'll be celebrating the 50th anniversary of NATO, the most effective defensive alliance in world history which kept the Soviet Union and its Warsaw Pact allies from attacking Western Europe for many decades. Now we have just accepted three new members into NATO, former members of the Warsaw Pact--Poland, Hungary, and the Czech Republic. What we should be doing on this occasion, if we had any sense, is abolishing the organization, that is, abolishing NATO, rather than adding new members, an action that gives the Russians fits as a threat to their own security. Of course our defense industries will prosper as these still relatively poor countries are forced to buy military hardware to meet their commitments to NATO. Where is President Eisenhower to remind us about the military-industrial complex? The mission of NATO was accomplished. The threat is no longer there. Why keep it going?

Well, things take on a life of their own, particularly if they support a large bureaucracy, a large infrastructure, and a large budget that buys lots of things from lots of folks. Like our own Federal Home Loan Bank, which should have been put out of business decades ago. Now NATO has to find new missions to justify its existence. Since it is no longer viable as a defensive alliance needed to ward off a military threat from a Soviet Union and a Warsaw Pact that no longer exist, it now seeks to intervene in conflicts in the Balkans, to send its troops into a sovereign state that doesn't wish to be invaded, to threaten governments that are mistreating their ethnic minorities, first with sanctions and then with bombings. What I am trying to say in an uncensored way is that we are in the process of converting a defensive alliance into what we think of as a peacekeeping force but that is actually prepared to commit aggression against a miscreant nation that has not attacked it or any other nation but that is behaving in ways of which we strongly disapprove.

I do not wish to belittle the important role that NATO played or its historical significance. But isn't it curious that there is nothing in this nation's capital of ours that is named after President Truman, or General Marshall, or Dean Acheson? Marshall didn't want anything named after him. I don't know that the other

21

two expressed an opinion. There is a campaign now being organized to name the State Department building after President Truman, now that most historians recognize that he was one of our greatest presidents. These men created the Marshall Plan (so named because Truman realized he was unpopular at the time, whereas Marshall was a hero, and he needed Congress to provide the money) and NATO, two of the greatest achievements of our foreign policy. Yet their names are nowhere commemorated in this city.[2]

Compare President Reagan, after whom a huge federal building and our National Airport have been named (I'll pass over in silence the question of Mount Rushmore). Actually, we should rename the Treasury Department building after President Reagan, for it is there that every year the folks have to refinance the trillion-dollar federal debt that Mr. Reagan left behind him. His administration was supposed to be promoting supply-side economics. In fact what they did was pump out that borrowed trillion dollars in additional demand, which fueled the buying binge that we have been engaged in for the past decade and a half and that has given us the biggest economic spurt in our history. Let us forget that that debt will be passed on to future generations. In time we will restore our normal inflation rate of 3 to 5 percent per year, and that debt, when it is paid off during the next century, will thereby become a much smaller proportion of our GDP, and therefore much less of a

---

[2] This deficiency was partly rectified in 2000, when the Clinton administration named the main headquarters building of the State Department the Harry S Truman building. Much earlier the largest auditorium inside the building was named after Dean Acheson. Perhaps there is something inside the Pentagon named for General Marshall.

burden in depreciated dollars. Thank God for inflation. Which brings me to:

Double-standard Civility: The Albanians of Kosovo are seeking independence, will probably have to settle for autonomy, at least initially, began rebelling when they had their autonomy taken away by the Serbs, and are now labeled terrorists by the Serbs. But we're not buying that, even though everyone has learned that you can win support from the U.S. government by labeling your enemies terrorists. Instead we're threatening to bomb the Serbs if they don't restore the Albanians' autonomy and allow us to fill their Kosovo province with NATO troops to enforce the agreement.

We are very selective in our attitude toward oppressed ethnic minority groups. Let's look at Turkey. That country's Kurdish population has never enjoyed autonomy, and after they began rebelling, their few rights to exercise their ethnicity were taken away. They began fighting for their independence a decade and a half ago, and would probably accept autonomy if it were now offered, to stop the bloodshed from which their people have suffered the most. The Turks label the Kurdish fighters terrorists and thereby win our sympathy and support. Instead of bombing the Turks we sell them all the weapons they want to put down this rebellion and cheer them on because they are fighting against terrorists. The Turks allow us to use their airfields to bomb the Iraqis and to protect the Iraqi Kurds from Saddam Hussein.

Turkey is our NATO ally and Serbia is not. The Serbs are the butchers of Bosnia. The Albanian Kosovars and the Kurds are both separatists, but they are trying to separate themselves from different masters. So that's why we resort to double-standard civility. Or is the difference perhaps that the Kurds live in the Middle East whereas the Albanians live in Europe?

Of course there are several kinds of Kurds. The Kurds in Turkey are bad Kurds because they don't want to be Turks. The Kurds in Iraq are good Kurds because they are not Arabs. They're good Kurds except when they're quarreling among themselves or collaborating with Saddam Hussein. Years ago they were even better Kurds when they were fighting against Saddam, and we gave them support until our friend the shah of Iran became concerned that they might detach his Kurds, at which point we dumped the Iraqi Kurds and allowed them to be subdued. So even double standards are flexible.

In realpolitik terms, rarely has a people been so used and then abused. The Kurds, over 25 million strong, are easily the largest ethnic group in the Middle East, or in Europe, or perhaps in the world, who do not have a state of their own. They were promised one after World War I, but that was not to be.

Our political and diplomatic leaders have been ignoring one of the most important axioms of the past half-century. It sounds simplistic, but it is fundamentally true, the essence of an axiom. It is this: "One man's terrorist is another man's freedom fighter. And one man's freedom fighter is another man's terrorist." I would add a corollary to that: "He who was once a terrorist can later become a respected national leader. And he who is a respected national leader may have once been a terrorist." Do you need examples? Nelson Mandela, Yasser Arafat, Menachem Begin, Yitzhak Shamir, Robert Mugabe, Joshua Nkomo. Mahatma Gandhi was an unusual person, to say the least. He is unique.

Certifying Civility: This applies to Mexico especially, and some other countries of Latin America and a few elsewhere. We have to certify that a country, Mexico for example, is cooperating with us in trying to prevent illegal drugs from being smuggled into this country. If we don't certify it, then we have to impose various sanctions, something we hate to do, as it would interfere with some very profitable trade. So we certify it, flying in the face of the facts as everyone knows them.

This could be called Hypocritical Civility, and that would be the proper term if you looked at the issue from the point of view of the other country. It could refuse to certify us. About what? About our failure to devote adequate resources to reducing the demand by Americans for these illegal drugs, the demand that makes the narcotics trade so profitable and next to impossible to control. So long as there is that great demand, the supply to satisfy that demand will get into this country by hook or by crook no matter what we do to try to keep those drugs out. We should be decertified for devoting so much of our funding, energy, manpower, and other resources to ineffective interdiction of drug smuggling and to incarcerating small-time drug pushers who are overflowing our prisons, and for devoting so little to the demand side, to treating addicts and educating our youth about the perils of experimenting with dangerous drugs. We don't deserve to be certified so long as we have addicts trying desperately to get into detoxification and treatment programs to kick their habits while we refuse to provide enough places to meet all of that demand.

Summit Civility: In recent decades a good deal of diplomacy--not the most useful kind, but often the kind receiving the most attention from the media--has occurred as presidents and prime ministers and other chiefs of state and chiefs of government have taken to meeting together from time to time to exchange views and palaver on a variety of subjects. This is pretty much meaningless talk, as the final communiques are always prepared well in advance and cleared by staffers with all parties concerned, which ensures they will be blander than bland. There was an exception to this rule at a summit held more than a decade ago in Reykjavik, Iceland, when President Reagan suddenly departed from his prepared script and suggested to his Soviet interlocutor that both sides abolish all of their nuclear weapons. This was not a joke and it threw the underlings on both delegations into a frenzy, since nothing unexpected is supposed to happen at such summits.

Last November there was a summit of APEC--it stands for Asia Pacific Economic Cooperation--in Kuala Lumpur, Malaysia. Some progress was made in dealing with the Asian financial crisis, though it was somewhat marred by the public attack on Japan's trade policies by our trade representative. But what was most unusual was an even more severe attack on the host of the summit, the Malaysian prime minister, by our vice president, who was substituting for our president. I have no idea whether his speech was written in the State Department, the White House, or campaign headquarters, but it was unlikely to have been State because it appeared to be aimed at a domestic American audience. The host was attacked on human rights grounds. The Malaysian prime minister is an autocrat with a bad record, and he deserves some criticism, because he's also a bad economist who blames his country's financial problems on currency speculators. But the thousand Asians in the audience were astounded to see such an impolite performance by the head of our delegation, who walked out of the dinner after his address before breaking bread.

The Malaysians saw the speech as encouraging demonstrators who were calling for the overthrow of the Malaysian leader. That might be a worthy cause, but the place and the time and the lecture violated all norms of diplomatic behavior, publicly insulted the host, showed disrespect for all the Asians present, and was in fact--as we say in diplomatic jargon--most counterproductive. I have it on good authority that the Asians are still talking about this incident months after the event, and citing it as demonstrating American arrogance and bullying tactics, throwing our weight around as "the only remaining superpower." We'll have to relabel this phenomenon as Summit Incivility.

Banana Civility: We are threatening all sorts of trade sanctions against certain European countries, trying (and if we get away with it, we will manage) to damage their exports of certain luxury goods to us. All because they have been favoring with subsidies the export to Europe of bananas produced by some of their poor former colonies in the Caribbean. If they eliminate these subsidies, as we demand, that will be the end of the banana exports from these small island communities, who will then, in order to survive, have to rely more on the trade in illegal narcotics and the fleecing of our tourists. The strange thing about this is that we grow practically no bananas ourselves--only a few in Hawaii--and export none to Europe. It's true that there's a gentleman living in Ohio who owns Chiquita Bananas, which are grown in Central America, and this gentleman spreads a lot of cash around in the form of campaign contributions to both Republicans and Democrats--lots of soft money, but a perfectly legal means of influencing our trade policies. This is extremely annoying to the Europeans, and it makes us look like both knaves and fools.

Our civility has now moved all the way from the sublime to the ridiculous, so on that unhappy note I will end these remarks.

U.S.-GREEK RELATIONS

In the ten minutes allotted to me I want to say something about two topics: so-called anti-Americanism amongst Greeks, and secondly, Greek foreign policy of the '80s and '90s as it has affected American interests.

I have long argued, I'm afraid not at all persuasively, that the question of anti-Americanism in Greece has been treated simplistically and misleadingly. Many Americans, whether or not they have visited Greece, believe that there is a lot of anti-Americanism in that country. The media are partly responsible for this, or perhaps mainly responsible, because the impression of anti-Americanism is strongest among Americans who have never visited Greece. They will cite things such as statements by Andreas Papandreou, or even that Margarita Papandreou used to march in the November 17 demonstrations directed at the American Embassy. Americans who visit Greece by and large experience no hostility toward themselves from those Greeks they encounter, unless they have the unfortunate experience of hiring a taxi driver who refuses to turn on the meter, feigning incomprehension, and then charges them, I should say overcharges them, perhaps $50 to get from the airport to their hotel.

Greeks are very sophisticated about distinguishing among people, countries, governments, and policies. Just because they may not like our policy on Cyprus, or

This talk was part of a seminar briefing held at the Meridian International Center on October 20, 1997, to assist Ambassador R. Nicholas Burns prepare for his new assignment to Athens.

because they believe we are favoring the Turks against the Greeks, because our government is pursuing policies they don't like, it is never translated into hostility to individual Americans or against the United States as a country, which to most of them is still an ideal country. Their animosity is directed against the government of the United States. If Greeks can afford it they send their children to be educated in this country's universities. I can't tell you what difficulty I had fending off all the Greeks who thought I could get their kids admitted to Athens College when they hadn't qualified otherwise, because Athens College, an American institution, was viewed as a ticket to get those kids into an American university, or even into a Greek university.

Greeks have emigrated to the United States in large numbers. You don't move permanently to countries you detest. Most Greeks view the U.S. in a much more idealized fashion than we Americans do ourselves. At the same time Greeks can become extremely upset by actions our government takes or by attitudes they perceive us as having, officially, toward their country. When they get angry at us they are acting in the manner of unrequited lovers, as rejected lovers. You don't get upset by being rejected by someone you don't love at all, by someone you detest. Greeks cannot understand why we appear to "love" the Turks. If we love the Greeks, they believe, we should detest the Turks. They can't understand how our government can neither love nor hate either one of those countries. That seems perverse and unreasonable, when the Greeks have justice on their side and the Turks do not. These relationships are viewed as black and white.

Unfortunately Greeks don't understand Americans very well either. They think we are all filthy rich, as well as naive, generous to a fault, and easily duped. That is a stereotype, but it is not hostility. So if you receive a ridiculously exorbitant bill after having enjoyed a nice meal in a Tourkolimano restaurant--sorry, Microlimani restaurant--don't chalk it up to anti-Americanism, but rather to exploitation of your naivete. You should have asked to see the menu, with the prices listed, and you should have asked, in advance, just how much that fish weighed.

A good deal of the alleged proclivity for anti-Americanism has fallen on the PASOK party and specifically on the head of the late Andreas Papandreou. It is true that he sometimes made statements that indicated a profound hostility for the United States. By Americans this was deemed particularly reprehensible, even traitorous, because Andreas had spent 20 years in this country and had been an American citizen.

But I can say based on many private conversations with him that although Andreas did have ambivalent feelings about the United States, in most respects his attitude was positive and admiring. He admired the relative classlessness of American society, our social and economic mobility, the dynamism of our economy--the most flexible and adaptable in the world--the readiness of Americans to welcome new ideas and new technologies, and a willingness to try them out, to experiment, our risk taking and our entrepreneurship, the magnificence of our system of higher education, both public and private, the more equitable treatment of women here than in most other countries, and perhaps most of all our devotion to democratic institutions and procedures and the rule of law. These are among the things that he hoped to instill in the Greek body politic when he went into politics.

What Andreas didn't like was his perception (not altogether accurate in my view) in the early '60s that the American government was heavily and wrongly involved in the internal affairs of Greece. This feeling was reinforced by the alleged role of our officials in the downfall of the Papandreou Center Union government headed by his father in the summer of 1965. Andreas wanted to liberate Greece from what he viewed as American tutelage. I must add that throughout his political career in Greece he had to counter the perception that he was an American interloper who had parachuted into Greek politics with his father's help, that he carried the baggage of having been absent from Greece during the war and German occupation, and that he was at least as American as he was Greek. This no doubt accounts in part for his effort to distance himself from the United States by being a vocal critic of some American policies. There are people in Athens to this day--I know some of them--who will try to persuade you that Andreas was really an American agent infiltrated into Greece by the CIA.

There did exist a more generalized anti-American sentiment among many quarters in Greece following the military coup of 1967 and the Turkish invasion of Cyprus in 1974, for which many Greeks blamed the United States. But this was really unfair and was a manifestation of Greeks' tendency to blame others for their homegrown misfortunes. Our crime in 1967 was not forcefully opposing the planned generals' coup that was preempted by the colonels, and our quiet acquiescence in the harsh dictatorship that followed, but I can assure you that we did not install Colonel Papadopoulos in power. He was a native product.

We did not stop the Turkish invasion of Cyprus, but the only way we could have done so would have been by intervening militarily, and that was simply out of the question. Cyrus Vance had warned us after he had defused the Greek-Turkish crisis over Cyprus in 1967 that the next time the Turks felt sufficiently provoked, they would invade and no power on earth could persuade them not to. Greeks tend to forget that it was their own government, headed at the time by Colonel Ioannides, that precipitated the debacle in Cyprus by overthrowing Archbishop Makarios and trying to kill him. And I wish to remind you that Greek anti-Americanism engendered by these events has always been directed against alleged failures by the American government, not by the American people, not by America as a country.

Now some brief remarks about Greek foreign policy and American national interests. My point is simply that the coming to power of PASOK and Andreas Papandreou in 1981 in time effectively eliminated foreign policy as a major factor in Greek domestic politics. Prior to that event there had been serious divisions over issues such as membership in NATO and the Common Market, over American bases in Greece, over relations with the Soviets and eastern Europeans, with the Arab states and Israel, over nuclear weapons and arms control, and military/security relationships in general, as well as how Greece should position itself in the East-West competition of the Cold War. As the PASOK government gradually modified its positions on these issues--forced to do so by the exigencies of being in power rather than in opposition--an unwritten and even unacknowledged consensus developed that harmonized the positions of the two major parties so that henceforth foreign policy virtually disappeared from the domestic political competition for election and governance.

There were of course still arguments about who could handle the country's foreign relations more effectively, but little discussion of issues as such. At the same time there was a consensus between the parties on the Cyprus issue, and relations with Turkey, which are of course central to Greece's national interests, though again politicians argued about who best could manage these problems. Later on splits developed, but mostly intra-party, over the Macedonian issue although not over Greek insistence on calling the country FYROM (the Former Yugoslav Republic of Macedonia), the Albanian collapse, and the breakup of Yugoslavia to some extent, but these questions did not impact severely on Greece's relations with its military alliance and economic union partners.

I believe it is not inaccurate to say that Greece now has a national foreign policy that is supported by most Greeks and is not a major partisan issue, which is not much different from the situation in the United States, where domestic issues predominate in our politics, and foreign policy does not play a major role, nor is even of much interest to our electorate at large.

And finally, although the United States and Greece do not always totally agree about how to deal with Cyprus, or how the Greeks and Turks should handle the problems between them, I think it is safe to say that harmonizing the foreign policies of the two countries--Greece and the United States--while always a basic function of diplomacy, will not be the overwhelming preoccupation of our new ambassador in Athens. As a footnote I would add that during my tenure in Athens, 1985 to 1989, my most difficult tasks related to negotiating a new agreement covering the four American military bases on Greek soil, and how to deal with international as well as local terrorism. The latter is still a problem, but the former--the issue of the American bases--has disappeared from the screen.

ATHENIAN DEMOCRACY

As I'm sure you're aware, I am a somewhat last-minute substitute on this program for Nick Burns, our ambassador in Athens. It's your loss, not mine. I'm very pleased to be here with you to help inaugurate this celebration, and to join with my friend, Ambassador Alexios Christopoulos, who himself will be substituting for his ambassador, Alexander Philon, who was unavoidably detained in Washington. I'm here because Nick Burns asked me to take his place after his boss, the secretary of state, ordered him to attend a conference of American ambassadors in Europe that conflicted with his appearance here. I used to work for other secretaries of state. Fortunately for me, she can no longer order me what to do. I'm retired.

It's your loss because Nick, whom I consider a friend, is much younger than me, in fact a whole generation younger. He's also much more energetic. And he is serving in Athens, and doing a superb job, which means that he's thoroughly familiar with what's going on there, whereas my service at that embassy ended a decade ago. But I do have one advantage. I'm not here to speak for the U.S. government. I can't and I won't. In retirement I can say what I want. This has been a great relief after 36 years of working for Uncle Sam.

One of the triumphs of American diplomacy in recent decades has been the spread of democracy throughout the world, with a concomitant emphasis on

This talk was delivered at the opening ceremony of "Homage to Greece--A Celebration of Hellenic Culture" at Binghamton University, New York, on October 7, 1999.

respect for human rights, as democratic regimes have replaced dictatorships and autocracies of the left and the right in many countries, whose peoples now enjoy liberties they never experienced before. Of course this has not been entirely due to the efforts of successive American administrations, but our commitment to spreading democracy, pursued more or less consistently over the past 50 years plus, has certainly played a role.

However, one of our failures, I regret to say, is that we have somewhat naively displayed an abiding faith that the cure-all is democratic elections that allow the people to choose their political leaders. Elections are certainly important, but they are not sufficient by themselves to install and entrench true democracy unless they are accompanied by the establishment of a range of democratic institutions and principles besides mere parliaments and elected executives. And I have come to believe that the most important of these principles is the rule of law, administered by an independent and incorruptible judiciary. Another error we have made, particularly with the formerly Communist-ruled nations, has been to believe that moving rapidly, even instantly, to a market-based economy can ensure the entrenchment of a democratic system. It is rather the reverse that will work: democracy first, market economy will follow.

We can see this problem in its most salient manifestation in the current situation in Russia, surely the most important country--one critical to the peace of the world--that has tried to transform itself from an unresponsive, unaccountable, arbitrary, and repressive authoritarian regime into a modern democracy. Yes, there is an elected executive and a national parliament, but the current state of affairs can most accurately be described as a kleptocracy whereby criminals have seized most of the economy and other levers of power and are ruling the nation in a lawless manner, and no one has recourse to courts that can enforce the few real laws that exist. Perhaps I am overstating the negative case, but I believe that in Russia the cart got ahead of the horse. The first and most imperative requirement after the demise of the Communist regime was not the urgent imposition of a market economy managed by so-called reformer-technocrats, but rather the establishment of the rule of law run by an independent judiciary and an executive capable of enforcing laws adopted by truly democratic procedures and elected representatives motivated by the wish to see the people prosper.

Which brings me to the major point I wish to make this evening, as it relates to Greece, and specifically to Athenian democracy of the classical period. Although our Founding Fathers were influenced by certain principles and beliefs that they found in the writings of philosophers of the Enlightenment, they were also steeped in the classics, both Greek and Roman. Even a superficial perusal of the official architecture prevalent in our national capital, and in many state capitol buildings, more Greek than Roman in style, will confirm what are doubtless the most significant original antecedents of our own democratic system. This was the democratic system invented, elaborated, and codified by the citizens of the city-state of Athens in the fifth century B.C. There is not time this evening to remind you of all the aspects of that extraordinary achievement, but I would like to make a few points about it.

The first is that democracy dawned in Athens with the work of the lawgiver Solon, who established objective property qualifications for the different classes of Athenian citizens. The subsequent history of Athenian democracy was the gradual extension of the franchise downward through these classes, so that an ever greater number of citizens were able to participate directly in politics and the governance of the city. It is true that Athenian democracy was defective, in that the franchise was not universal. For example, women were not permitted to participate in politics, and the economy depended on the institution of slavery. But it would be anachronistic to dwell on these matters. Women did enjoy certain important rights other than attending the assembly, and the slaves were enemies defeated in battle but spared their lives, not people of another race torn from their roots and transported in chains across the oceans. We should acknowledge with some shame that slavery was not abolished in our own country until nearly a century after our founding, and women did not receive the vote until another half-century later.

At the next stage in Athens the political reformer Ephiàltes replaced rule by an oligarchy of aristocrats with a complex democratic system that enshrined the rule of law, and assigned the creation of the laws and their execution to popular assemblies of the mass of citizens. Since it was impractical to hold mass meetings of the entire citizenry for every issue that arose, a council, or in Greek the *voulì*, was instituted, made up of 500 citizens chosen by lot for one-year terms to meet regularly. Thus was representative government invented, and what is the real mother of all parliaments. These men were truly amateur legislators, not professional politicians. There were term limits: no citizen could serve more than twice in his lifetime. Members were paid a stipend, to compensate them for lost work-time. Decisions about war and peace were now made by those who would risk their lives in the fighting if the decision was to go to war--what an innovation!

The courts were staffed by ordinary citizens, again chosen by lot. People accused of crimes were assured that

37

their peers in status, not upper-class magistrates, would render the judgments. Athenians took the administration of justice very seriously, and handled it themselves instead of turning it over to professionals or a caste. In the assembly every citizen, whether eloquent or unlettered, had the right to speak. The system was one man, one vote. All citizens gained experience in governance. The parliament changed its composition every 12 months. Nothing was done in secret. A written record was kept. There were no document shredders in Athens, and the laws were inscribed on stone.

There was no standing army or navy. All citizens could be called upon at any time to serve. Generals and admirals were elected, not chosen by lot, and they were held accountable for the results of their campaigns, with dire consequences for failures. I should add that ambassadors and other official negotiators with foreign powers were also elected from among those deemed qualified, not chosen by lot.

The Athenians invented a much more sophisticated means of removing leaders from power than our cumbersome, debilitating, and fractious impeachment process. It was called ostracism, a word derived from the practice of using a broken bit of pottery (*òstrakon* in Greek) as the ballot paper in this procedure. Once each year the assembly decided whether or not to hold an ostracism. If the vote was in the affirmative, and following a 70-day cooling-off period, the actual ostracism vote was scheduled and on the given day any citizen could come to the marketplace, or *agorà*, and scratch on a broken piece of pottery the name of the person he wished to have ostracized. Provided that at least 6,000 valid *òstraka* were handed in, the man with the highest count against him was compelled to leave the province of Attica and not set foot therein again for 10 years. While absent in exile he could still, however, receive the income from his property in Athens.

This was the manner invented for getting rid, temporarily but for a long time, of a leader or politician who had become too unpopular or who was considered a danger to the state. There was no indictment, no trial, no speeches for or against, just a straightforward expression of the popular will through balloting. Archaeology has produced the interesting fact that in one urn that served as a ballot box were found 191 òstraka inscribed with the name Themìstocles, but the handwriting was from only four different hands. This would indicate several possibilities, one being electoral fraud or ballot stuffing, and another being that the pottery ballots had been prepared in advance by anti-Themìstoclean forces for distribution to illiterate voters who could not prepare their own òstraka.

There was a case when the procedure of ostracism was subverted, and revealed a basic flaw in the system, which perhaps explains why this was the last recorded use of ostracism. In around 416 B.C. it was generally accepted that either the "hawk" Alcibìades or the "dove" Nìcias (their opposed positions relating to war or peace with Sparta, Athens' archenemy) would be sent off into exile through ostracism. But their supporters collaborated and turned the tables on their common enemy, Hypérbolus, who thus received the most votes and lost the election, which sent him into exile instead. The result was that the conflict between the hawks and the doves remained unresolved, and ostracism was never again resorted to, probably because the citizens had lost confidence in its ability to do the job it was meant to do.

Another imaginative innovation of the Athenians was a procedure by which any citizen could bring an indictment against another citizen for allegedly introducing to the assembly a proposal that was either invalid in form or substantially in conflict with an existing law. If found guilty by a court the perpetrator was fined. This procedure discouraged the introduction of frivolous or pernicious proposals that at the very least wasted the precious public time of the good citizens of Athens. Our own Congress should take note.

I wish I could go on with the to me fascinating story of these original democrats in Athens, but my time has expired.

PROBLEMS IN INTRA-BALKAN RELATIONS

I trust it's understood that I wasn't invited to speak to you here today as a spokesman for official American policy toward the Balkans, or on any other topic that may come up in the question period. I believe U.S. policy toward the Balkans during the past decade is fairly well-known to the public, although explanations of and justifications for that policy have probably not been as well articulated as they might have been.

What I will be doing now is offering a commentary on that policy, actually a critique of it. The salient event in that region has of course been the breakup of the Yugoslav Federal Republic. This has created instability in the region, great suffering for literally millions of people, not to mention the deaths of tens of thousands, the displacement of many more into the status of refugees in their own country or abroad, and great destruction of the infrastructure in the former Yugoslavia as well as of the homes of countless families.

Much of this tragedy could have been avoided, I believe. At first the United States considered that this was a European problem, to be solved by Europeans without our own involvement. The Europeans failed to act in a timely fashion, and even exacerbated the situation by the premature official recognition of breakaway states without considering the consequences. The breakup

---

This lecture was delivered on April 4, 2000, to the students in a Learning in Retirement Institute course on foreign affairs at George Mason University in Virginia. Certain portions that repeat material in "Civility in Diplomacy" have been excised.

of Yugoslavia was probably inevitable, but it could have been managed differently. The ethnic tensions were perhaps too strong to keep a federation together, but I believe a timely and forceful intervention by the major European powers could have insisted on the protection of minority rights and lawful residence in states created to enclose a dominant majority ethnic group.

What could have been done--and it will be said this is hindsight, although I and others made the suggestion early on--would have been to convene a conference of the major European powers and the United States and Russia, along with the leaders of the various Yugoslav ethnic groups, as well as the leaders of Yugoslavia's Balkan neighbors, in the manner of the Berlin Congress of 1878 but with an expansion of participants. That Congress dealt admirably with an earlier major crisis in the Balkans and resolved a large number of problems without resort to war. I cannot be as admiring of the work done on the Balkans at the Paris Peace Conference in 1919, which redrew the borders of the Balkan states in profound ignorance of as well as disregard for the ethnic demography of the region, for example in assigning parts of the Albanian population to four different states.

A new Berlin Congress at the beginning of the 1990s would most likely have resulted in the redrawing of boundaries in the region to reduce the potential for conflict among ethnic groups. I am fully sympathetic with the Greek government's strong opposition to changing any state boundaries in the Balkans on the sound principle that the populations are by now so mixed ethnically that it is impossible to create ethnically pure states, that all states have minorities within their borders, and that opening up the matter of borders would encourage widespread irredentism and therefore conflict. However, a fairly minor restructuring of the borders within the former Yugoslavia, agreed upon with the consent of all parties, and accompanied by an entrenched commitment to the protection of minority rights, could have prevented the open warfare and ethnic cleansing that ensued from the breakup.

The European powers declined to deal with the issue of the breakup of Yugoslavia and the bloodshed and ethnic cleansing in Bosnia, in the early stages when foreign intervention might have been successful. One could say that the non-intervention policy of the Europeans was an effort to keep things from getting worse, but it ignored the suffering of those being ethnically cleansed.

But we were also guilty of apparent indifference as the crisis in Bosnia led to increased bloodshed. Initially, we thought the Europeans would or should take care of this problem, but they didn't. Germany was partial to the Croats and Slovenes; Russia, France, and Greece were partial to the Serbs; only Turkey (among NATO powers) was partial to the Bosnians, but it had to stay out, as the Bosnian Muslims were a leftover from the years of the Ottoman occupation. Who helped the Bosnians? Iran, a rogue state from our point of view. We dithered while the atrocities and systematic ethnic cleansing horrified the world. This was a place for some dedicated diplomacy at least, but by the time we stepped in the situation was almost beyond repair.

When the U.S. government finally engaged itself directly in the Yugoslav situation, the result was the much-praised Dayton Accord, the handiwork primarily of Richard Holbrooke. What he did at Dayton, Ohio, was to force the contending parties in and around Bosnia to agree to a settlement that none of them actually wanted, and that they are sure to subvert, sabotage, and overturn when they get a chance. Nevertheless it was a major achievement in that it established a truce and stopped the bloodshed among the Serbs, Croats, and Bosnian Muslims, which had cost many lives and major displacements of people, at least for some time. That was about all that could be achieved at that time. But it also effectively ratified new borders separating the principal ethnic groups that resulted from the despicable ethnic cleansing for which all shared some responsibility, but which the Serbs (led by the war criminal Slobodan Milosevic) had initiated. It created a new and recognized status quo. Even though the fighting has stopped, very few refugees have been able to return to their homes, so it appears that the ethnic cleansing is irreversible, and in effect has been condoned. A few of the worst war criminals have been brought to justice, but some of the perpetrators of the worst atrocities--those who gave the orders--have escaped any punishment.

Why did it take us so long to decide to intervene in the Balkan imbroglio? For my birthday last year a friend gave me a copy of Robert Kaplan's book about the Balkans, now available in paperback. It's called *Balkan Ghosts*, and was published in 1993. I put it aside, as I had not liked Kaplan's earlier article and book about the so-called Arabists in the State Department, in which he had quoted me out of context, and whose theme was that the Arabists controlled our policies toward the Middle East region in a manner detrimental to the interests of Israel, when in truth these Arabists have been notable for having had minimal influence on our policies, as their expertise has mostly been ignored.

I did recently read the portion of the new book devoted to Greece, and decided I could skip the parts about the other Balkan states he visited. Kaplan lived in Greece for seven years, including the four-year period when I served as ambassador there. His account is so biased and misdirected, because he disliked intensely the democratic leadership that ruled Greece during that period, principally on ideological grounds, that his book lost all credibility for me. The indispensable book about the Balkans remains Rebecca West's classic *Black Lamb and Grey Falcon*, published in 1941.

The curious fact about Kaplan's book is that it apparently had a major impact on American policy toward the Bosnia problem at the very highest level of decision making in our government. In his foreword to the paperback edition he writes that the book "acquired a public policy significance" that he never intended. He reports that "in 1993, just as President Clinton was contemplating forceful action to halt the war in Bosnia," he and his wife read *Balkan Ghosts* and "the history of ethnic rivalry ... reportedly encouraged the President's pessimism about the region, and ... was a factor in his decision not to launch an overt military response in support of the Bosnian Moslems, who were being besieged by Bosnian Serbs." Kaplan points out that there is little about Bosnia itself in the book, and he is disconcerted because he was himself a hawk about Bosnia and publicly advocated American intervention including military action in support of the Bosnian Muslims. He does not claim that ethnic harmony and peaceful relations have predominated in the Balkans, but he believes that outside intervention to stop the bloodshed was definitely called for early on and he said so publicly at the time. My comment is that perhaps we should ask the White House press office, in addition to publishing the president's daily schedule, to inform the press and public what books, if any, the president is currently reading.

There is not time today to address this entire question of ethnic conflict in the Balkans, but I would like to point to four salient aspects of this geographic region.

They are history, geography, religion, and land. First history. Until fairly recently in their histories most of the Balkan peoples were ruled by foreign powers for centuries. Prior to World War I, the Greeks won their independence in 1830, and the Serbs gained some autonomy from the Ottomans about the same era, but independence came later on. Statehood for the Bulgarians came only in the anti-Ottoman Balkan wars of the latter part of the 19th century, and for the non-Serbian parts of Yugoslavia and for Albania only after World War I. Prior to these events most of the Balkans were divided between two empires, the Austro-Hungarian and the Ottoman.

Geography. This is a very mountainous region. (In fact, the word "balkans" in Turkish means "mountains.") This has meant that ethnic groups were isolated from each other and from other ethnic groups, with very little interaction for centuries. People lived close to home, traveled little, and often knew nothing of people in neighboring valley systems. Strangely, a river system was the most important dividing line in the region. It is natural but destructive to use rivers as boundaries between political entities, because rivers are means of communication, not barriers to it. Peoples living on both sides of a river can communicate with each other easily with boats, and therefore people of the same tribe or ethnic group live on both sides of a river. Mountains are much better places to draw borders, because mountains are obstacles to travel and therefore divide peoples. This phenomenon is pronounced in Africa, where many national boundaries follow rivers and other bodies of water, which are actually unifiers, not dividers. In the Balkans the division between the Ottomans and the Austrians was for a long time the Danube and Sava River systems. They create a prominent line on maps of the region. Three Yugoslav capitals are river towns: Zagreb and Ljubljana on the Sava, and Belgrade where the Sava joins the Danube.

Religion. That same line was generally a religious division. To the north of the line the people were and are Catholics, to the south Eastern Orthodox Christians or Muslims. The Serbs, Greeks, Macedonians, and Bulgarians are Orthodox; the Croats, Slovenes, Hungarians, and others are Catholic. The Albanians and the Bosnian Muslims are Muslim, converted during the times of Ottoman rule. And the Turks are of course Muslim. Common religion was one of the forces that unified people of disparate ethnicity, especially under foreign rule, which was often by people of a different religion. One need only point to the religious wars that often devastated Western Europe for centuries (and still do today in some places, for example Northern Ireland) to not be surprised that religion has played a major role in conflicts in the Balkans.

Now land. It is difficult for Americans to appreciate the strong pull of an attachment to land, to specific land, to a specific piece of land. Land is about all that poor people have to sustain their existence. If one loses it one dies. If someone tries to take it away from you, you will put your life on the line to protect it, to keep it. We are a new population on this continent, and do not have centuries of attachment to specific pieces of land. And we are mobile--we buy and sell properties and move around the country with amazing speed. That is not the way of the Balkans. The same family may have been living on a plot of land for many generations.

I own a tiny piece of land, about a half-acre, on a Greek island on which I built a modest village house as a summer retreat. I have the only existing deed to that land. The farmer from whom I bought it had no document proving he owned what he was selling. But he told the notary who drew up the deed that it had been in his family for as long as anyone in the village could remember, and no one came forward to contradict him. No one bothered with deeds during the nearly 400 years of Ottoman rule over Greece. People owned and worked the land that had always belonged to them, and no one dared question that. The tragedies that have visited Yugoslavia in the past decade are compounded by the immense violations of people's attachment to their land.

To return to recent Balkan history, we and our European allies in NATO eventually became engaged in the Kosovo conflict. Anyone knowledgeable about the Balkans could have predicted a decade ago that the most explosive situation affecting Yugoslavia would eventually erupt in Kosovo, because there it was not a minority that was being oppressed, but a majority population of close to 90 percent. Nothing was done in the years following Milosevic's 1989 abrogation of the Kosovo Albanians' precious autonomy. When they eventually rebelled against this oppression, and it was clear that Milosevic was planning and already beginning a brutal ethnic cleansing of the province, the U.S. and its European allies stepped in. Given Milosevic's record of repeatedly starting wars and encouraging ethnic cleansing in the disintegrating former Yugoslavia, some sort of intervention was certainly called for.

The major NATO powers made a valiant but misguided and mismanaged effort at the Rambouillet conference to defuse the situation diplomatically to prevent further bloodshed. There were several flaws in that diplomatic effort. The first was attempting to achieve a compromise between two contending parties treated as more or less equal, whereas one party was a sovereign government dealing with part of its own population and territory while the other party was a liberation movement rebelling against that government and seeking independence, an outcome everyone except the KLA (the Albanian rebels), but including the mediators, opposed. The rebels bought the proposed agreement; Milosevic did not, understandably.

He was asked to sign an agreement that would have had the effect of giving up part of his country's territory, something no Yugoslav leader, even a shining democrat, could ever have signed voluntarily, certainly no leader whose main claim to power was his undiluted nationalism, whose political popularity was based on his long-standing anti-Albanian policies in Kosovo. Milosevic was also asked to allow a NATO force--not an international peacekeeping force authorized by the United Nations Security Council--to occupy that territory as well as all of Yugoslavia, I repeat, all of Yugoslavia. Again, no Yugoslav leader could have agreed to such an imposition. Thus there was no prospect of that proposed agreement averting a war. Our diplomacy failed utterly, and NATO, led by the U.S., resorted to bombing Serbia proper, Kosovo, and also Montenegro.

It was a grievous error to abandon our diplomatic effort at Rambouillet and to turn on our war machine. A deal was possible that would have avoided all the bloodshed, destruction, and misery. The key elements of a compromise would have been a demand that Milosevic restore the Kosovars' autonomy that he had taken away from them in 1989, a cease-fire on the ground in Kosovo, the insertion into Kosovo alone of an international (not NATO) force of well-armed peacekeepers with a UN Security Council mandate to stop all oppression of the civilian population of Kosovo and to carry out the disarmament of the KLA fighters or their expulsion from the country if they refused.

That is a deal that Milosevic would have bought,

and that the KLA would have had to accept because they would have had no other choice. It would have been consistent with the policy of no border changes. And it would have averted a war. What was wrong with what we offered, and was bound to be rejected by Milosevic, was the coupling of a guaranteed independence for Kosovo after three years with an invading NATO force imposed on a sovereign country and member of the UN with no controlling mandate or international supervision. Milosevic aside, no Serbian leader could have been expected to agree to sign away a part of his country's territory and to accept a foreign occupation that would eventually guarantee the dismemberment of his state.

The diplomatic solution we tried was misguided and overly ambitious, an attempt to obtain a country's acquiescence to a redrawing of its borders by outside powers backed by their overwhelming military superiority. The only mystery is how any experienced diplomat could have expected to achieve such an outcome through persuasion. It was a classic "non-starter" that did not provide a compromise of the interests of the parties involved in a manner consistent with the correlation of forces on the ground. And, it must be added, that flew in the face of the history of the Balkans, which no one seems to have bothered to take into account. So a war took over when diplomacy failed.

Who won the war over Kosovo? The Clinton administration, supported by its close ally in Great Britain the Blair administration, claims that it won the Kosovo war because it gained the three primary objectives of that war, namely, (1) the Serbian military and police forces out of Kosovo, (2) a NATO peacekeeping force into Kosovo, and (3) the Albanian refugees back home in Kosovo. That is quite true, so far as it goes, but we must also face up to some of the other objectives that were not achieved, and some of the unintended collateral consequences of that war.

Here are some. The Milosevic regime remains in power in Belgrade, and by all accounts despite the bombing and heavy sanctions it seems to be more entrenched than ever. There is less democracy in Serbia now than there was before the war, as Milosevic has suppressed most opposition media. Milosevic is no doubt a brutal opportunist and inhumane scoundrel, a war criminal and whatever else we wish to call him, but he is also a Serbian nationalist who knows how to exploit the feelings of his people to support himself against his and their enemies.

Does anyone recall another recent war that caused us grief because we did not understand that its brutal leadership could count on the nationalist sentiments and determination of their people to prosecute a war against overwhelming odds despite the sacrifices required to obtain their liberation from foreign domination, as they saw it?

Some of the Serbian infrastructure destroyed by the bombing has been rebuilt, but the Serbian populace still suffers undue hardship and can't find a way to get rid of Milosevic. Rather than maintaining a multiethnic population in Kosovo, the end result has been that most of the former Serbian population has fled or been driven out, leaving behind an almost purely Albanian province. And although our policy was to oppose redrawing any borders or breaking up the rump Yugoslav state still further, the present situation seems likely to result in an independent Kosovo republic, at least temporarily, and perhaps a move to create a greater Albanian state to include Kosovo, which would have dire consequences for Macedonia with its minority Albanian population and would create further instability for the whole region.

51

Finally, what about our NATO peacekeepers? How long will they have to remain in Kosovo? How many years will it be? Or how many decades? And at what expense? The Serbs have a long historical memory, and they still consider Kosovo sacred Serbian territory. They have repeatedly harked back to the year 1389, when the Ottoman Turks defeated the Serbian army in Kosovo, but an event that the Serbs consider a valiant effort to maintain self-rule, an event celebrated in their national folklore. Will the Serbs simply bide their time until the peacekeepers leave, and then invade Kosovo and seek revenge against the Albanian population that drove them out?

One could make the argument that Milosevic, the indicted war criminal, was the actual winner of the war in Kosovo. In the agreement that stopped the bombing he obtained a commitment that Kosovo will remain part of the sovereign state of Serbia. It brought an international rather than a strictly NATO force of peacekeepers into Kosovo, including a Russian contingent. And instead of NATO command and control it provided a UN Security Council mandate and supervision over that force, meaning that countries sympathetic to Serbia--Russia and China--can, if they are willing, use their veto powers to protect Serbian interests in the province of Kosovo.

None of these provisions were offered to Milosevic at Rambouillet, thus giving him grounds to reject that agreement. Ironically, it required months of bombing to put them on the table. Instead what he was offered by our misguided diplomacy at Rambouillet was the eventual and certain loss of a province of Serbia to independence.

The question to be posed to Milosevic is whether the cost of the destruction of Serbia and Kosovo wreaked by NATO was worth the benefit of these gains. It seems doubtful, for he paid a very dear price for what he gained. The three wars he started against Croatia, Bosnia, and Kosovo created a huge displacement of Serbs from large areas where they lived--for example, in the Krajina region of Croatia, around Sarajevo in Bosnia, and of course Kosovo--Serbs who have become refugees, displaced persons, in Serbia itself. That tragic outcome was the direct result of Milosevic's policies, so he can hardly be termed a winner.

But what about our side? If our diplomacy had been as skillful as we think it was we could have obtained from Milosevic at Rambouillet the agreement that ended the bombing and avoided the costs we have paid and the misery subsequently inflicted on Serbs and Kosovars alike. Those who managed our diplomacy at Rambouillet have a lot to answer for.

My conclusion is that neither side won the war in Kosovo. It was a strange war without victors or vanquished. Our bombing solution took a very bad situation and made it even worse. This was not a military failure. It was a failure of our diplomacy to find a way to avoid war.

What our diplomats and war planners neglected to take into account before starting a campaign to bomb the Serbs into submission was that when this operation was over the various peoples inhabiting the region would still have to learn to live together in the same neighborhood, next door to each other, as good, peaceful neighbors. All of the ethnic groups involved--the Albanians of Albania, the Kosovars of Albanian ethnicity, the Macedonians both Slavic and Albanian, the Montenegrins, of course the Serbs, and people living not far away including the Greeks, the Bulgarians, and the Hungarians, and the former Yugoslavs in Bosnia, Croatia, and Slovenia--all of these people are going to have to continue to live in that very same neighborhood, next door to each other.

How do we think they will get along with each other in the future? Will the Serbs and the Albanian Kosovars be able to live together, even next door to each other, in peace? Will the Albanians and the Macedonians be able to co-exist with their neighbors the Serbs? What about the Montenegrins, and the Serbs of Bosnia, and their neighbors the Bosnian Muslims and the Croats?

Of course we will have to assist in reconstructing all the terrible damage we have wreaked on that neighborhood from the air. We will have to rebuild Serbia, and Kosovo, and Montenegro, as well as Macedonia and Albania, which were ravaged by the influx of so many hundreds of thousands of destitute refugees. Has anyone estimated the probable cost of this Marshall Plan for the Balkans? Besides all the physical destruction and loss of life, all areas involved have been damaged severely both economically and socially--not only Serbia but Kosovo itself, as well as Albania and the Macedonian Republic, and Montenegro. The whole area has been destabilized.

There will now be a long and costly rebuilding exercise required. We wanted to stop the ethnic cleansing and we opposed Kosovo independence. The ethnic cleansing was even worse than we expected, and independence is now the probable result, at least in theory, though it may trigger renewed conflict unless we plan to stay in Kosovo forever.

Perhaps of equal importance, the Kosovo operation damaged our relations with both Russia and China, the two countries most important to our own national security and that are central to our aim of preserving world peace. Both those countries, unlike any in the Balkans, are nuclear powers. The Russians opposed our bombing the Serbs but also didn't like the precedent of outside intervention into domestic conflicts, mindful of their own problems with Chechnya and other troubled regions. But they also apparently learned the wrong lesson from Kosovo and applied it to Chechnya.

Charles Krauthammer is not one of my favorite columnists--I agree with him perhaps 10 percent of the time--but in his column published a few days ago that I have distributed to you, he makes the case that the person who learned from Kosovo that it is acceptable and effective to use brute force to suppress a rebellion was Vladimir Putin. He put down the rebel Chechens brutally, gained immense popularity with the Russian people for doing so, has got himself elected president as a result, and now we will have to live with this former KGB spy as our Russian interlocutor for the next four years.

The Chinese also opposed our actions in Kosovo, primarily because they saw it as a foreign intrusion into a domestic problem and the use of military might to impose a solution. The accidental bombing of the Chinese Embassy in Belgrade threw a monkey wrench into our always problematical relations with that country. Our difficulties with China are now focused on the Taiwan Strait, but our ability to negotiate with its very tough regime was not enhanced by that accident.

I should note that differences over policy toward Kosovo adversely affected relations between Greece and the United States to some degree, although mutual membership in the NATO alliance and the strong ties that have been fostered on both sides during the post-World War II years served to mitigate the disagreements.

There have been even larger consequences than on our relations with individual countries. The Kosovo operation has set a precedent that is brand new in international law. It is that if a group of countries (for example, NATO's members) decide that a sovereign country is oppressing some of its own people to an unacceptable degree, then it is lawful for those countries to attack that nation, to make war on it, to get it to change its behavior. Heretofore such authorization required UN Security Council action. Since such a resolution risked being vetoed by Russia and/or China, NATO didn't go to the UN.

As for NATO, the Kosovo project was apparently an effort to establish for itself a new role in Europe that would justify its continued existence, as well as its expansion eastward to the borders of Russia. In the process NATO transformed itself from a strictly defensive organization designed to protect its members from attack into an aggressive force to be used to impose its will on non-members who are misbehaving by its lights.

This transformation, and the fact that the U.S. played the overwhelming military role against Serbia, have caused the European members of NATO to ask serious questions about the precedents set and what the future may hold for the alliance and their membership in it. The perhaps foreseeable result has been that the European members of NATO have begun the planning to create an independent military arrangement, a strictly European one independent of Washington. The military weaknesses of the Europeans that were displayed in the Kosovo operation, with most of the missions requiring American forces, have caused the Europeans embarrassment, as well as concern that American views have overwhelming weight in NATO decision making. He who has the best weapons obviously has the loudest voice.

One justification for what we did in Kosovo, this one a favorite of pundits rather than policymakers, was that NATO's "credibility" was at stake. It's regrettable that we did not take advantage of the celebration of NATO's 50th anniversary not long ago here in Washington to abolish the organization. NATO had achieved its mission of protecting Western Europe from military attack by the Soviet Union and its allies in the Warsaw Pact. There was no reason to continue its existence, to try to find new missions for it to prolong its life, especially missions not covered by its charter, outside its geographic area of responsibility, and to turn it from a defensive alliance into an aggressive attacker of a sovereign state that had not attacked it and was not a threat to NATO itself or to any of its members.

There was even less reason to expand NATO eastward, to the detriment of our relations with Russia. NATO was not created to carry out humanitarian missions and is ill-equipped to do so. It was created and organized to defend against and defeat an attacking military force, not to inflict wholesale damage on a country unable to defend itself against an overwhelming attack.

Finally, Kosovo was the first war in our (or anyone's) history with a strategy designed and tactics used to ensure that all of the casualties and suffering would be endured by the people, military and civilian, being attacked--that is, the Serbs--and the people they were oppressing--the Kosovar Albanians--while there would be absolutely no casualties on the attacking side--our side--or as close to zero as possible. That can hardly be a definition of a just war for a moral cause.

To conclude on a more positive note, I should say something about recent developments in relations between Greece and Turkey, which have taken an interesting turn. One important development not much commented upon was the advent of George Papandreou as foreign minister of Greece. He is the U.S.-educated son of former Prime Minister Andreas Papandreou, and is of moderate temperament, without the visceral hang-ups about the Turks that afflict many Greek politicians.

He was formerly deputy foreign minister and got the top job after his predecessor, the mercurial Theodoros Pangalos, had to resign over his mishandling of the Ocalan affair--the capture by the Turkish government of the leader of the Kurd rebellion in Turkey while he was in Greek custody in Kenya. I predict that George Papandreou will be a future prime minister of Greece, and in the meantime he has been the point man on the Greek side in trying to improve relations with Turkey.

The change in the atmosphere between these two rivals that border on the Aegean Sea came about through what became known as "earthquake diplomacy." In August of last year Turkey suffered a severe earthquake in the northwest, and the Greeks dispatched a team of crack specialists to help rescue trapped victims, recover bodies, and comb through the rubble. This had great resonance in Turkey as a kind humanitarian gesture that had no ulterior motive other than to help people in distress. Three weeks later Greece suffered a similar earthquake, though not as severe, centered in the suburbs of Athens. The Turks reciprocated by sending to Athens a team of Turkish rescue specialists to help deal with the aftermath. This exchange of earthquake helpers, well publicized by the media in both countries, especially on TV, seemed to create a breakthrough of good feelings on both sides. It led to an exchange of visits by the Greek and Turkish foreign ministers--the first such exchange in 38 years--and the beginning of talks by technical teams to address the long-standing issues between Greece and Turkey relating mainly to the Aegean, such as the territorial sea, the continental shelf, airspace rights, disputed islands, and so forth.

Thus far this has not extended to the Cyprus problem. A few not terribly important but symbolically significant bilateral agreements have been signed, and there is some hope that the more complex and serious issues can now be addressed in a climate of compromise. The Greeks took a major step forward by welcoming, rather than vetoing, the decision taken by the European Union leaders meeting in Helsinki to welcome an application by Turkey to join the Union at some future date. Were NATO members Greece and Turkey also to be fellow members of the EU, it would help strengthen bonds of peace and cooperation between these two nations that are neighbors who are destined to live next door to each other, like it or not.

On another level, just last week the mayors of Athens and of Istanbul were in Washington at the same time and both addressed a lunch hosted by the Western Policy Center that I attended. It was clear that these two mayors have their own dialogue going to promote cooperation between Greeks and Turks, particularly in the business sector. Interestingly, they also revealed that there is an organization made up of the mayors of the capital cities of all the Balkan states, including Belgrade, Sarajevo, Tirana, and Skopje, whose governments may not be on good terms but who see no reason why their cities should not try to cooperate.

One last point. The mayor of Athens revealed that his city now harbors 800,000 illegal immigrants, most of them Albanians, but including Kurds, Afghans, Iraqis, Iranians, and Africans. Some are economic refugees rather than victims of war or oppression, but this gives you an idea of the scope of the displaced-persons problems of that region of the world.

THE MIDDLE EAST PROBLEM
HAS BEEN SOLVED

The Middle East problem--otherwise known as the Arab-Israeli conflict--has been solved. The only remaining obstacle is that the participants in the current peace talks, and their friends around the world, have not yet realized that fact. What could remove that obstacle and push the negotiations to a final resolution would be an important change in U.S. policy toward the issue that is long overdue.

This may sound like a thoroughly unrealistic proposition so soon after the guns have fallen silent following a week-long devastating and entirely disproportionate attack on southern Lebanon, and in the wake of Secretary of State Warren Christopher's most recent exercise in shuttle diplomacy around the capitals of the Middle East, a trip required to patch together, once again, the frayed fabric of the "peace process" before it totally unraveled. But it is a fact that the conflict is ripe for resolution and the elements needed for a solution should be apparent to all parties.

For four and a half decades there have been two main hindrances to peace between the antagonists, between the Arabs and the Israelis. One has been the

---

This op-ed article was written on August 9, 1993, and was rejected for publication by several prominent newspapers. It was written before anything was known about the Oslo Accord being negotiated in Norway (a major intelligence failure by the United States) and exactly five weeks before that agreement was signed at the White House. It is published here for historical reasons.

refusal of the Arabs to recognize the legitimacy of Israel and its right to be accepted as a normal and permanent member of the state system of the Middle East region. But today that is no longer an issue. Egypt has signed a peace treaty with Israel, and that country's other Arab neighbors--Lebanon, Syria, and Jordan--are now negotiating directly with the government of Israel toward the same objective, that is, peace treaties. By any measure these Arab states have recognized Israel *de facto*, and the conclusion of peace treaties will transform that status into *de jure* recognition.

Even the most important non-contiguous Arab states are on board, notably Saudi Arabia. Recently a leading Saudi personality with long-standing anti-Zionist credentials remarked to me: "Throughout our history we have always had important Jewish communities in the major cities and centers of the Arab world. Now we will have an even larger one in our midst, and it is called Israel!"

Conditions are ripe for peace on all of the frontiers of Israel--provided that Israel adopts wholeheartedly the basic principle of the current negotiations, which is the "land for peace" formula. Israel's reluctance to do so has been the other major hindrance. We need to end the sterile debate over the significance of the absence of the article "the" from in front of "territories occupied" in UN Resolution 242, which all sides agree is the basis for the negotiations. An especially strong statement of principle in the same resolution emphasizes "the inadmissibility of the acquisition of territory by war." This means that Israel cannot legally acquire *any* of the territory it occupied in the 1967 war simply by claiming it as war booty. All of it must be relinquished unless the peace treaty negotiators agree to make some territorial adjustments.

In return, all of the neighboring Arab states must make peace--a full and undiluted peace--with Israel within its pre-1967 boundaries. Resolution 242 recognizes the right of all the states "to live in peace within secure and recognized boundaries," which is an essential but somewhat redundantly phrased formulation, given that the only secure national boundaries are those that are recognized by a state's neighbors.

The easiest current negotiation is that between Jordan and Israel. Jordan has been ready to make peace with Israel for many years. The territorial disagreements between these two states are few and small, and easily resolved. All that holds up a peace treaty is agreement on the other fronts.

Despite the recent horrendous events in southern Lebanon, the Lebanese front is also easily resolvable, for Israel has made no territorial claims on that frontier, despite its occupation of a "security zone." What Israel seeks is absolute security from attack. Full return to Lebanese sovereign control, withdrawal of the Israeli armed forces, demilitarization, a major UN peacekeeping presence, and removal of all rival militias from the frontier area can create a permanent peace between Lebanon and Israel. Most Lebanese, and presumably all Israelis, want nothing else. Probably Israel will have to make provision, within Israel, for the Lebanese Christian surrogate army of the south that cannot be reintegrated in Lebanon.

The formula for peace between Syria and Israel is already on the table. Syria demands complete Israeli withdrawal from the Golan Heights (phased if necessary), while Israel demands full peace by Syria. Each side insists that the other lay out all of its cards first. The U.S. could mediate this impasse by simply collecting the cards held by both sides and displaying them together on the table.

The two hands are likely to match. Game over. Peace treaty follows.

In case the Syrian and Israeli positions turned out not to be identical, the U.S. would be required to mediate the differences. It is an axiom of mediation technique that it is easier for both antagonists to make concessions to a third-party mediator than to its opponent. Thus each side could accept compromises proposed by the U.S. mediator that it might feel compelled to reject if proposed by its antagonist.

The one remaining unresolved area is of course the Israeli-occupied West Bank and Gaza Strip and their Palestinian populations. The international community at large is responsible for the absence of a solution to this issue, which should have been settled long before the 1967 war that resulted in Israel's occupation of these territories. The error was the failure to insist on full implementation of UN General Assembly Resolution 181 of 1947, which called for the partition of Palestine into separate Jewish and Arab states and the internationalization of Jerusalem. The decades-long inability of the Palestinians to exercise their right of self-determination is at the heart of this problem, but even here there are serious negotiations underway with the Israelis to determine the future of the Palestinian-inhabited territories and of the Palestinians as a people.

Unfortunately these talks have been making minimal progress. There is a growing realization that the "Madrid formula," the ground rules established for the 1991 Madrid conference that launched these negotiations, was fundamentally flawed in two major respects. First, the negotiations were forced into two stages, with the first stage limited to talks about Palestinian autonomy under continued Israeli rule and occupation, while postponing--until three to five years later--decisions about the final status of the occupied territories, and neither stage guaranteed to implement the Palestinian right of self-determination, since the final status is to be negotiated between the two parties rather than decided by the Palestinians whose territory is at issue. Second, despite any nuanced promises made to the Palestinians by the American hosts, Jerusalem was excluded from the discussion, at the insistence of Israel, in the face of the indisputable fact that East Jerusalem is occupied territory by any definition of that term. In the absence of a solution to East Jerusalem, there is no outcome acceptable to the Palestinians, nor to the Arab and Muslim worlds generally.

This explains the lack of progress. The "autonomy" offered to the Palestinians by both the Shamir and Rabin governments is what those in the occupied territories dismiss as "mukhtar autonomy," meaning the kind of governance they enjoyed in centuries past under Ottoman rule, by village headmen who can determine what hours shops can be open or what days the garbage is collected but who have no powers to resist the creeping annexation of Palestinian lands and resources in the territories by settlers and the Israeli authorities who support them. Such "autonomy" provides some control over people, but not over land, water, and other resources, and amounts to voluntary acceptance of subservience. The precedent is the Bantustans of South Africa.

There is no way this problem will be resolved without the exercise of Palestinians' self-determination, with whatever option they choose, whether an independent state, federation or confederation with Jordan, or with Israel, or with both, or some other arrangement. The Palestinian right of self-determination is not something to be negotiated. Rights are not negotiable, especially with a negotiating "partner" that for

64

years denied there was Palestinian people or Palestinian land or Palestinian rights. The most serious error in U.S. policy on the "Palestine problem" for many years has been the insistence that the solution lies in negotiations between Israelis and Palestinians. Given the great disparity in power between these two antagonists--a disparity that owes its dimension to the intervention of the United States--the U.S. insistence on "negotiations" lacks honor and justice as well as rationality.

It is here that the U.S. must act, by changing its policy stance dramatically and expressing its absolute support for Palestinian self-determination, even if the result might be an independent Palestinian state in the West Bank and Gaza. This change in U.S.policy could be the impetus that will encourage enlargement of the trend in Israeli public opinion toward majority acceptance of the idea of a neighboring Palestinian state. Arguments against this idea because of the "mortal danger" to Israel such a state would pose have fallen into the dustbin of ridicule with the end of the Cold War and the *de facto* recognition of Israel by all of the major players in the Arab world.

The U.S. should at the same time end the fiction that it isn't engaged in a dialogue with the PLO. It has been talking directly with the PLO ever since James Baker began the shuttle diplomacy that led to the Madrid conference, and in fact Israel has been dealing with the PLO through its representatives at the Washington peace talks, despite all pretenses to the contrary. For an Israeli-Palestinian settlement to be viable it must be presented to the two constituencies by people with political credibility before those audiences. In the case of the Palestinians that means the PLO.

What is needed now is for someone (the U.S. is the only available actor) to give the parties a strong push into making the hard decisions that must inevitably be made but that they have all been trying to avoid in the hope that the U.S. would "deliver" the other side. The U.S. should make clear that it will not choose sides but will push both sides. Equally.

If this sounds as if Israel is destined to make the important concessions to ensure a successful outcome on the Palestinian-Israeli track, consider what concessions the Palestinians have already made. They have accepted Israel's right to exist on about 78 percent of the land of Palestine that they always considered their own, now populated by millions of people who immigrated from distant lands to displace millions of indigenous Palestinians. And they have already agreed to establish their own state on the 22 percent of the land remaining, which is less than half of the territory they were allotted 45 years ago by the international community in the 1947 UN partition plan. They are also probably prepared to accept serious limitations on the sovereignty of their state, for example its demilitarization.

This brings us to the thorny final issue: Jerusalem. The U.S. says a solution should be negotiated by the parties. Israel says the issue is not negotiable; Jerusalem will be the eternal, undivided, sovereign capital of Israel, period. The Palestinians say East Jerusalem has been their own religious, cultural, commercial, and political center for centuries. The U.S. has compounded its own misguided approach by relegating the decision about Jerusalem to the final stage of negotiations, a position that ignores its centrality to the basic dispute. A failure to resolve Jerusalem satisfactorily risks bringing the whole "peace process" to naught. Jerusalem should be put on the table today.

Israel's claim to exclusive possession of Jerusalem is based on bad history and worse politics. Yes, Jerusalem is the city of David, but it is also the city of Jesus, and of Muhammad. It is a city sacred to hundreds of millions of people, perhaps 2 billion people worldwide. The Jews are hardly the only people with irrefutable religious, emotional, cultural, and historical ties to the city. Exclusivity cannot be justified, and will only lead to tragedy.

The ideal solution--given these unique circumstances--was the internationalization proposed by the UN in 1947. But that solution is today unacceptable to both the Israelis and the Palestinians, the primary antagonists whose conflicting claims must be reconciled. The most promising outcome would therefore appear to be a plan for shared or joint or dual sovereignty, under which the city would remain undivided, would contain the capitals of both the Israeli and the Palestinian states, and would be maintained as a demilitarized city open to all the peoples of the world, of all faiths or none, a haven of peace and harmony, and a light unto the world. The Jews would be sovereign in Jerusalem, and so would be the Palestinians--as well as everyone else, in the one place on earth where questions of sovereignty would no longer be a cause for human conflict, a city dedicated to peace and reconciliation.

"GAZA-JERICHO FIRST" IS ONLY
THE BEGINNING

The term "Gaza-Jericho First," used to describe the Israeli-Palestinian agreement signed at the White House on September 13 [1993], is not exactly a misnomer, but it does not adequately express the vast scope and significance of that agreement. Limited Palestinian autonomy and self-rule are to begin in those two parts of the occupied territories within three months of the signing of this "Declaration of Principles," following negotiation of an interim agreement that, among other things, will call for accelerated withdrawal of Israeli military forces from Gaza and Jericho, to be completed within a period not exceeding four months after the signing of the interim agreement.

But the Declaration looks well beyond that timetable. It provides for the election by the Palestinians (including those residing in Jerusalem) of a governing Council "in order that the Palestinian people in the West Bank and Gaza Strip may govern themselves according to democratic principles." These are to be "direct, free and general political elections" that "will constitute a significant interim preparatory step toward the realization of the legitimate rights of the Palestinian people and their

---

This article, here included for historical reasons, was published in The San Diego Union-Tribune *on September 19, 1993, six days after the signing of the Oslo agreement at the White House, and again in the November/December 1993 issue of* The Washington Report on Middle East Affairs. *That is more than eight years ago.*

68

just requirements." The stated goal is for elections to be held no later than nine months after the entry into force of the Declaration, or 10 months from now. And no later than the eve of these elections, Israeli military forces will be redeployed outside the areas populated by the Palestinians. The Palestinian police force to be created "will insure public order" during the elections, which will be held under international observation. After the inauguration of the Palestinian Council, the Israeli civil administration "will be dissolved, and the Israeli military government will be withdrawn." That means the end of the Israeli occupation for the Palestinians inhabiting these territories.

These procedures clearly contemplate the establishment of a Palestinian government whose jurisdiction "will cover West Bank and Gaza Strip territory." Although the Council will not have jurisdiction over certain major matters--specifically Jerusalem, settlements, military locations, and Israelis living in the territories--these issues are to be settled in the "permanent status" negotiations that are to begin in two years and conclude at the latest in five years, when the interim arrangements will expire. These negotiations will also deal with the Palestinian refugees, security arrangements, borders, relations and cooperation with other neighbors, and "other issues of common interest."

Those in Israel who strenuously oppose this deal negotiated by Prime Minister Rabin's Labor government are no doubt correct that it will lead inexorably to the creation of a Palestinian state in the West Bank and Gaza, but they are mistaken in believing that there is any alternative solution to Israel's Palestinian problem. Israel will not be able to live in peace and security until the Palestinian people have exercised their right of self-determination, a right recognized by the international community as far back as the 1947 United Nations Partition Plan. The deal reached between Rabin and Arafat will achieve that aim. The result may well be a confederation between Jordan and the Palestinian state, but only after the latter has been created and the Palestinians have chosen to join with Jordan in some sort of mutually beneficial union. The critics on the right in Israel who argue that a Palestinian state would be a "mortal danger" to Israel are contradicted by the realities of power relationships in the Middle East in this post-Cold War and post-Gulf War era. The challenge for both Israel and the international community will be to assist the Palestinian state to become a viable entity, not to check its military power, which is likely to be nil.

What is most remarkable about the recent events in the Middle East peace process is not so much the agreement signed at the White House but the exchange of letters between Rabin and Arafat that constituted mutual recognition by Israel and the PLO. That was the indispensable precondition to the interim and final status negotiations to come, although anyone predicting such a development at this time would probably have faced derision. The logic of it is evident, at least now. The Labor Party leadership apparently came to the realization that the only way to reach a workable peace agreement was to deal with its leading antagonist, the PLO, for decades vilified and ostracized as a "terrorist organization," because only the PLO had the stature and organization to deliver on whatever it agreed to. An elementary principle of negotiation is that you must deal with your antagonist, and the other party must have credibility with its constituency to make any deal struck salable. Israel, after many months of negotiating with surrogates for the PLO, and maintaining the fiction that it was not dealing with the PLO, finally realized that direct dealings were the only path to peace.

This was the major concession that brought about this historic compromise, and it was made by Israel. The PLO has also made concessions, but they are minor by comparison. Arafat, in writing, has recognized Israel as a legitimate state with a right to live in peace and security, has renounced terrorism and other acts of violence, has accepted UN Security Council Resolutions 242 and 338, and has committed the Palestinians to try to obtain their rights through negotiations. But as far back as December 1988 Arafat made all of these commitments in a speech to the UN General Assembly; they were never subsequently repudiated. In the years since he has also agreed by implication that Israel cannot be rolled back from its 1967 borders and that what the Palestinians seek is a state in the West Bank and Gaza alone (22 percent of historical Palestine), certainly not the "liberation of Palestine." The only really new elements in his most recent declarations are two: a promise to rescind the articles of the Palestinian Covenant that deny Israel's right to exist, and a promise to bring the *intifada* to an end. The former is mainly a paper exercise, and the latter will become irrelevant 10 months from now, for if there are no Israeli troops patrolling in Palestinian population centers by then, no Palestinian kids will be throwing stones at them.

The single concession by the Israeli side in this exchange between Arafat and Rabin was what made the historic breakthrough possible: the government of Israel recognized the PLO as the representative of the Palestinian people and agreed to negotiate peace directly with it. Implicit in this simple statement is the recognition that the Palestinians are a distinct people, with rights, and in this context the most important right of self-determination.

71

There is a quite amazing asymmetry between the amount of compromising each side has had to do and the relative power positions of the antagonists. The Israelis, with the most powerful military machine in the Middle East, with the unstinting backing of the world's only superpower, in physical possession of all the territory in dispute, and without great public pressure at home to make peace if it risked the security of the state, have made the single concession that was hardly predictable. The Palestinians, as divided and disputatious as ever, led from exile, with the PLO losing popular support in the occupied territories to extremist rejectionist factions such as Hamas, bankrupt in the aftermath of the Gulf War, with no hope of challenging Israel militarily, and with a weakened political position even in the Arab world, could be expected to make concessions, so long as they were not as fundamental as abandoning their wish for their own state. Perhaps the lesson is that the weaker party cannot make major concessions because that only makes it weaker, while the stronger party can afford to concede because it retains its relative strength even after the concession.

What seems to have won out on both sides was weariness with the unending and costly struggle and a desire for peace, not at any price, but at an acceptable price, along with a mutual recognition that this was probably the last chance for peace in the lifetimes of the leaders on both sides. And both sides were concerned that extremists, who prefer continued conflict to peace, were gaining ground.

With the Palestinian problem in process of resolution, the peace treaties between Israel and its other Arab neighbors that have been under negotiation for the past 22 months should move forward rapidly. The result will be the *de jure* recognition of Israel by all the Arab

72

states and its acceptance into the state system of the Middle East as a normal and unexceptional member. Jordan and Israel have already agreed on the agenda for their peace negotiations. They have no major disputes, and progress was impeded solely by the impasse on the Palestinian track. As for Syria and Israel, the makings of a deal are present and are self-evident: full Israeli withdrawal from the Golan Heights (perhaps in phases) and normal peaceful relations with Syria. These have been on the table for some time, but the antagonists have engaged in an Alphonse-Gaston charade of who would speak first. There may be a delay because of psychological overload in Israel. As for Lebanon, no territorial claims are at stake, only security issues, and with peace breaking out all over, the necessary arrangements should not be difficult to conclude.

An interesting question is why the U.S. was left on the sidelines while Norway refereed the secret talks that have made possible the resolution of this century-old conflict. One can only hazard a guess. Of all the principal players in the Middle East peace process, Washington is probably the leakiest. Realizing how necessary it was to maintain secrecy, especially so as not to enable the extremist enemies of peace on both sides to sabotage the deal after premature disclosure, both the Israeli and Palestinian leaderships apparently opted to leave Washington in the dark because Washington can't keep a secret. But more than that, the PLO has justifiably been irritated that Washington has held it at arm's length and even terminated its earlier dialogue with the PLO on irrational grounds. For good reason, Washington has not been noted for its evenhandedness in dealing with the parties to this dispute. As for the Israelis, they also bristle at pressure from Washington, which, though long a loyal patron, can behave in ways that appear patronizing.

Probably Rabin decided that if he was going to make concessions, he would make them on his own, not because someone told him it would be necessary. Ultimately, however, the important thing is not who gets the credit, but that peace is now in process.

TO END THE VIOLENCE

In its May 20 [2001] op-ed piece "To End the Violence," *The Washington Post* offered a forum for Dennis Ross to provide his analysis of the situation between Israel and the Palestinians. After a decade of failure to convert the "peace process" into "peace" while trying to keep it alive as a mere "process," Ross's views are definitely passé. Furthermore, his op-ed piece demonstrated the uneven-handedness of our approach to the problem for the past decade and beyond.

The fundamental flaw in his presentation was to posit an equivalence between the violence attributed to the Palestinians and the violence engaged in by Israel. Both sides are supposed to renounce violence and get back to the peace table. Renouncing it or denouncing it would be fine, but ignores the differences in motivation between the two sides.

The Palestinian violence is an expression of the extreme frustration that drives people to extreme actions such as suicide bombings after decades of suffering occupation, oppression, and destructive violence by the occupiers of their territory, who are seen and experienced as nothing but oppressors and violators of their human and property rights.

This article, written on May 23, 2001, having been rejected by The Washington Post, *was subsequently published in the October 2001 issue of* The Washington Report on Middle East Affairs. *Interested readers can find other letters and op-ed pieces rejected by* The Washington Post *at www.watchpost.org.*

Terrorism is a tactic that is resorted to out of weakness, by people who have no other means of expressing their extreme frustration. Any potential terrorist would much rather be able to mount an F-16 and shoot rockets at his perceived enemy, but that option is not available to him. He would much rather invade his perceived enemy's territory with a tank and shoot up a police station than blow himself up at a bus stop. Terrorists targeting civilians are seeking revenge, admittedly, but the means they use are not because they are deranged, but because they have no better choice.

This terrorism is the work of individuals and groups who are not under the control of the Palestinian Authority. If they were wise they would realize that their actions are not advancing the cause of the Palestinian people but are rather resulting in further oppression of their fellow civilians. But after so many years of suffering oppression they are beyond wisdom.

It is thoroughly misguided for officials like Ross and their sympathetic pundits to argue that Arafat is condoning the violence by his side in an attempt to force concessions from the Israeli side, or to pressure the international community "to intervene and rescue him." Arafat cannot end the violence by his side. Given the frustration of his people, he would be overthrown-- probably killed--if he seriously tried to stop the violence. One major fallacy of the Oslo Accord is that by it Israel tried to force Arafat and his Palestinian Authority to police the occupied territories, as well as to prevent frustrated Palestinians from attacking Israelis inside Israel, when Israel itself, with all of its police and military assets and firepower, had been unable to do so during the previous *intifada*. That was an unrealistic requirement.

By contrast, the Israeli violence against the Palestinians, presented as an effort at deterrence, is similar, though not equivalent, to what it is receiving--that is, "retaliation" if one wishes to be polite about it, "revenge" if one does not. It is not proportional to what it has been receiving, not solely in terms of the numbers killed, but in terms of firepower directed at civilians.

The most fundamental point, however, is that it is state-initiated, state-directed violence using the armed forces of the state to inflict the violence. Thus it is totally controllable by the authorities, not uncontrollable as in the case of Arafat. It is not the expression of frustrated Israeli citizens (except in fairly rare cases such as Baruch Goldstein's attack on the worshipers in Hebron's Ibrahimi mosque). And when it includes using air power in often successful attempts to assassinate individuals on the Palestinian side, we are dealing with state terrorism and war crimes.

This is where people like Ross ignore the great disparity between Palestinian violence and Israeli violence. There is no equivalence, either in motivation or in execution. Sharon confirmed this when he offered to stop the violence on his side if the Palestinians would reciprocate. The point is he can order it to be stopped by his side, because his armed forces are his; Arafat cannot, because he does not command the suicide bombers on his side. He could tell kids to stop throwing rocks, but he cannot stop suicide bombers from blowing themselves up. The only equivalence is that the Israeli government could not stop a fanatic from assassinating Prime Minister Yitzhak Rabin.

Ross was correct that Israel's primary goal is to "get security and a normal life" for its citizens (but in fact Israel wants a lot more than that). Israel already has the means to achieve that primary goal, and without reaching any bargain with the Palestinians. However, it is unrealistic to expect that to happen under the current

77

regime in Israel. The following would achieve that Israeli goal immediately: cease the occupation of all of the Arab territory occupied in the 1967 war (Gaza, the West Bank--including East Jerusalem--and the Golan), withdrawing all its armed forces, dismantling the settlements, and repatriating all of the settlers back to Israel. Israel could then close its borders to all of its neighbors, including the Palestinians, and, if necessary, build a wall or a fence to keep them out.

Israel would then become an isolated enclave in the Middle East--but that is what it has already become, through its own actions and its unwillingness to reciprocate the acceptance of its existence by Egypt, Jordan, and the Palestinians (in the Oslo Accord). This would be a tragic outcome, but if all Israel wants is security and a normal life, that is the way to achieve it. If it wants acceptance, then it must learn to respect that its neighbors have rights as well.

The fact is Israel has no right to hold on to any of the territories occupied in the 1967 war. Journalists would do well not to adopt, as they have, the Israeli term "captured," as if that meant that the Israelis now possessed this land--that is, owned it--and could dispose of it as they wished. It is "occupied," not "captured," land, and there is no justification for staying there, annexing parts of it, changing the demographics through massive settlement of their own people, and even claiming the right to negotiate its future sovereignty. These are actions prohibited by international law as well as by U.N. Security Council Resolution 242, which has been the basis for all efforts to resolve the conflict, and which includes the inadmissibility of the acquisition of territory by war.

The Israelis' contention that these territories are "disputed" also won't wash. Only they are disputing the ownership. No one else is. If they wish to insist on that

78

point, then the Palestinians would be justified in "disputing" the ownership of the land of Israel itself. In sum, Israel has no right to decide the ultimate fate of the occupied territories.

The actions proposed above--ending the occupation, withdrawing from the occupied territories, and dismantling the settlements--not only would give Israel security and a normal life for its citizens, but would fully implement what international law and the international community have long called for. There is no need for negotiated agreements with any other parties. Unilateral actions by Israel would solve the problem once and for all. The Arabs have learned that Israel is too strong militarily to be challenged by armed force, and they would leave it in peace. The Palestinian grievance dating from 1948 would be dissipated, and everyone in the region could get on with their lives.

Utopian? Hardly. The now defunct "peace process" was utopian, in trying to resolve in any other way the inevitable struggle over ownership of a small piece of land by two peoples, each having what they believed to be a legitimate claim to the exclusion of the other.

TRYING TO DEFINE TERRORISM

My assigned topic is "Trying to Define Terrorism." It might be regarded as unwholesome and perhaps indeed unpatriotic to take up such a subject while we are engaged in a "war against terrorism," but as it appears that that war is likely to be extensive as well as prolonged, with no discernible limits in space or time, it seems even more important than ever that we try to understand just what this phenomenon is that we are waging war against. For some people it may be upsetting at this juncture to try to examine the problem dispassionately, that is, objectively. But emotional reactions can lead to very bad decisions. We need definitions that go beyond slogans such as "One man's terrorist is another man's freedom fighter," and "Terrorism, like beauty, lies in the eye of the beholder." True as these formulations may be, they risk getting us bogged down in a semantic quagmire. It doesn't help either when some in the media, like Reuters and CNN, decide to avoid use of the term "terrorist" in order not to be judgmental!

In an op-ed piece published in *The Washington Post* on October 5 [2001], columnist Michael Kinsley, editor of *Slate* Internet magazine, argued that trying

---

This talk was delivered as part of a discussion on November 29, 2001, at the Center for International Policy on the overall topic "The List of Terrorist Nations: Useful Foreign Policy Tool or Flawed Instrument?" It was published in the American Academy of Diplomacy's Diplomatic Agenda *issue of December 2001, and in the* Middle East Policy *issue of March 2002.*

to define terrorism is impossible and in some cases (for example, Osama bin Laden) is actually absurd, though it is, as he said, a problem. He called media avoidance of use of the term "terrorist" an exercise in moral relativism. He noted that the Justice Department's draft anti-terrorism bill defined terrorism to include "injury to government property" and "computer trespass," much too broad coverage in his view. And one congressman complained that the bill could define terrorism to include bombing an abortion clinic, a definition that would not strike many other people as unreasonable. President Bush has made the goal of his war to be victory over terrorism of "global reach," a presumably practical rather than a moral limitation, Kinsley pointed out. But such a victory, he wrote, is unlikely for "terrorism is like a chronic disease that can be controlled and suppressed, but not cured."

Kinsley's piece made some other worthy points. A major problem is how to have a definition that you apply consistently. This was a major industry in our government in the 1980s, when a definition was badly needed to explain why we were supporting a guerrilla movement against the government of Nicaragua and doing the opposite in El Salvador. Can "terrorism" mean acts of violence in support of political goals except when committed by a government? "This sounds deeply cynical, but makes a lot of sense," Kinsley wrote. But how about "state-sponsored terrorism"? This leads to a "hopeless conceptual muddle if non-government is the key to defining terrorism." Perhaps one could use "tactics aimed at civilian non-combatants rather than professional soldiers." All of these definitions are flawed or inadequate, Kinsley argued, because "they leave out people you wish to include, and they include people you don't think deserve the term 'terrorist.'" The most accurate definition, he concluded, may be the famous statement about defining "obscenity" offered by Supreme Court Justice Potter Stewart, who said he couldn't define obscenity, but "I know it when I see it." This, however, would rob the term "terrorism" of its moral power, as well as its propaganda value.

Earlier this month my friend John Whitbeck sent me an email in which he argued that the word "terrorism" (and here I'm quoting him) is "so subjective as to be devoid of all meaning but, at the same time, extremely dangerous because people tend to believe that it does have meaning and use and abuse [the term 'terrorism'] by infusing it with whatever they hate as a way of avoiding rational thought and discussion and excusing their own outrageous behavior. The best way to win the 'war on terrorism' [Whitbeck continued] would be through an international treaty banning use of the word."

So let us try to be rational. The first point to be made is that terrorism is not an ideology. Nor is it a political program or a project. It is a tactic. To repeat: it is a tactic used to achieve certain aims. It is a means to an end, not an end in itself. Terrorism and freedom fighting are two quite different things. Terrorism is the indiscriminate use of violence against--generally the killing of--civilian non-combatants in pursuit of a political aim. Freedom fighting is a program or a project, such as the national or ethnic liberation of a territory, or the overthrow of a regime deemed to be oppressive, as in a civil war. Freedom fighters may or may not use terrorism, though they often do.

There is a rare and special category in the history of terrorism that is indeed revolutionary, but also anarchistic or nihilistic rather than programmatic (for example, the Nechayev variety--named after one of its principal perpetrators--used in 19th century czarist Russia to assassinate people), whose purpose was destructiveness against hated objects with little hope of effecting any political change, with no positive program at all, simply to harm and disrupt the state and the society as much as possible. The idea was to destroy order and peace, to attack the regime, with no possibility of replacing the existing social order and governance with anything deemed better, but rather replacing order with anarchy. This species of anarchistic terrorism exists in a contemporary setting as well, the best known, to me at least, being in Greece, where anarchist terrorists known as "November 17" have succeeded in assassinating 23 prominent individuals over the past 26 years, including four American officials, creating a certain amount of mayhem but with absolutely no hope of making any changes in the regime or its policies. Japan, among other countries, has also experienced this kind of terrorism.

We need to make a further distinction based on who uses the tactic of terrorism. In the context of a war that is not between nation-states it is used either by revolutionary insurgents attacking an existing regime or by that regime itself, the incumbents, to protect itself from being overthrown. Terrorism is also used in nation-state wars, for example in the wholesale and indiscriminate bombings of civilians living in cities--a tactic used by both sides in World War II, culminating in the atom bombings of Hiroshima and Nagasaki, a deliberate and successful attempt to end the war quickly by threatening the extinction of populations. How acute the problem of definitions is becomes manifest when anyone who tries to explain the atom bombings as acts of state terrorism in wartime is pilloried as anti-American if not worse.

There are a few things that are new about contemporary terrorism, but there is a lot that isn't new.

Allow me to hark back 31 years, to November 1970, when I took a seminar in modern warfare taught by the late Professor Klaus Knorr at the Woodrow Wilson School of Princeton University. Each student had to research, prepare, and present a term paper on an assigned topic. Mine had the fancy academic title of "Approaches to a Theory of Terrorism as a Mode of Revolutionary or Counter-Revolutionary Warfare." There was a dearth of scholarly literature about terrorism at that time. I gathered everything available in the Princeton library system, and it was all listed on a one-page bibliography. The paper began by listing 42 countries that had experienced terrorism since World War II. I would like to summarize some of the findings in that paper, which began by trying to define terrorism and not succeeding any better than I will today. I will skip over all the examples and just try to state the major principles. At that time most of the conflicts in which terrorism had played a role were either civil or anti-colonial struggles.

The most useful definition I found was this one: "a symbolic act designed to influence political behavior by extranormal means, entailing the use or threat of violence." This is useful because it stresses the symbolic nature of the act, the political (rather than military) nature of the goal, and the extralegal nature of the means. In a civil context, the incumbents use enforcement terror, while the insurgents use agitational terror. It cannot be stressed too much that on the insurgents' side, terrorism is the tactic of the weak. For them terrorism is highly efficient, because by attacking symbols of the state using very limited resources they can dramatize the vulnerability of the state and the ability of the terrorists to disrupt and partially destroy the state at some of its vital centers. The psychological aim is to strike fear among the attacked population. Thus the most effective means are indiscriminate attacks against civilians, which can break down confidence in the state's ability to provide security.

Much of the earlier literature was in French and grew out of research into the use of terrorism in the Algerian liberation struggle. In that case, and others like it, the targets were not "innocent civilians" from the point of view of the Algerian freedom fighters, but hated "colons"--colonists who were all deemed guilty of resisting the independence struggle. The point here is that the victims of terrorism may be perceived as "innocent" by themselves and their compatriots, but quite otherwise by the terrorists attacking them. On the matter of the terrorist using that tactic out of weakness, here is one example. Following his arrest, the FLN chief in Algiers was quoted as follows: "I had my bombs planted in the city because I didn't have the aircraft to transport them. But they caused fewer victims than the artillery and air bombardments of our mountain villages. I'm in a war, you cannot blame me."

From a position of weakness, terrorism is extremely economical of resources. Insurgency is cheap, counter-insurgency costly. "Merely by making anonymous phone calls warning of bombs planted in luggage, the insurgents can disrupt civilian airline schedules and scare away tourists." To jump ahead for a moment to Osama bin Laden, compare the assets and resources available to the United States with Osama's assets and resources. The disparity was enormous, as has just been demonstrated. So why did Osama employ terrorism? Because, given the paucity of his resources when compared with those of his target, that was his best option, perhaps his only option. He attacked us out of weakness, not strength. The goal, in somewhat technical terms, is to alter dramatically the power equation in the terrorist's favor.

A primary aim of terrorism is advertising and publicity for the terrorists' cause, whatever it might be. This is very effective in countries such as the United States with its free, open, and highly developed media. A secondary aim is to weaken morale on the attacked side and to build up morale on the attacking side. Terrorist acts display resolve and daring among adherents of the terrorists' cause, despite being viewed as cowardly by those on the targeted side. In some cases terrorism is at least partially intended to provoke reprisals, for when a regime defending itself against terrorists ends up killing innocent bystanders, sympathy can bring recruits to the side of the terrorists. Making the defense against terrorism very costly for the governing regime, especially in anti-colonial struggles, can cause the incumbents to abandon the fight and allow the insurgents to win. There are many examples: in British experience alone we have Ireland, Palestine, Malaya, Cyprus, Kenya, and others.

I do not have time to get into terrorism used by the incumbent side to protect itself, but believe me that it has been used extensively, usually ineffectively, and often in self-defeating ways, because the greatest advantage held by a government being attacked by terrorists is that it practices the rule of law, and has as its primary purpose the protection of the security of its citizens and the preservation of public order and a peaceful society. I will make one point: the most effective tactic against terrorist groups, proven by much evidence and history, is to penetrate them with agents in order to obtain intelligence about their membership, their aims, their tactics, and their plans. This is not impossible to do if the terrorist organization is bent on recruiting new adherents in order to expand its membership, influence, and power, but it can be costly and dangerous in terms of human lives.

To move to the contemporary scene briefly, what is unchanged about the terrorism we have recently experienced and what is new about it? We are still dealing with weak terrorists acting to change the power equation dramatically. September 11 was a perfect illustration of changing the odds. In the end Osama bin Laden may well lose his life and his organization may be thoroughly diminished, though it is unlikely to be completely destroyed. But look at what he accomplished, especially after comparing the assets that he commands with what the United States commands. The terrorist acts themselves were utterly horrible and tragic, directed against innocent civilians who became the principal victims, but Osama succeeded in getting us to start a war. By using 19 fanatics, a relatively small amount of money, and some clever planning and tactics, he killed more than 3,000 civilians who were related to perhaps 100,000 other people, displayed our vulnerability in myriad ways, damaged our economy, boosted unemployment nationwide, disrupted the world's premier financial center, sowed fear amongst much of our populace, made himself the number one international terrorist, and caused us to change a great many things in the ways we live our lives. People are afraid to travel on airplanes, even though the odds against ever being on a hijacked airliner are in the range of at least a million to one. Some people are now afraid to travel at all.

And he has done this by bringing major terrorism to our own soil. That is what is very new. Terrorism in the form of mass murder of Americans, however, is nothing new. It has been going on in the Middle East for many years. There was the bombing of our embassy in Beirut in 1983, and the bombing of our Marine barracks in Beirut later in 1983 that caused President Reagan to pull our forces out of Lebanon, no doubt the objective the terrorists had in mind. There was the Khobar barracks bombing in Saudi Arabia, the objective of which was to drive our armed forces out of that country, Osama's prime aim. Then there was the attack on the USS Cole in Aden harbor last year, again an attack on the presence of our armed forces in the Arab world.

Our embassies in Nairobi and Dar es Salaam were chosen as targets for truck bombings because they were easy targets, easier than attacking us on our own soil, but those embassies were symbols and elements of our presence abroad and of our power throughout the world, and many Americans were killed as well as many more Kenyans and Tanzanians. Some of these later attacks were apparently the work of Osama and his group. Regarding the East African embassy bombings, Madeleine Albright indelicately stated (as quoted in *The Washington Post*), "This is hard to say and I haven't found a way to say it that doesn't sound crass, but it is the truth that those [attacks before September 11] were happening overseas and while there were Americans who died, there were not thousands and it did not happen on U.S. soil." So much for the views of the former boss of our diplomats who risk their lives while serving abroad. The earlier victims were government employees and our military personnel. Presumably they are supposed to expect to be attacked by terrorists. What we have had now is attacks on American civilians on American soil by foreign terrorists for the first time. What is new is a change of geography and a change of victims, and both have been shocking to our people.

(The *Post* article in which Secretary Albright's quote appeared had the headline "How Afghanistan Went Unlisted as Terrorist Sponsor." It highlighted some of the absurdities of this project of labeling certain states as supporters or sponsors of terrorism, the topic of our session today.)

Osama's primary objective is to drive our armed forces out of the Arab world, particularly Saudi Arabia, and to end our political and financial support of Arab regimes he would like to bring down, such as those of Saudi Arabia and Egypt. Osama is not the first to target a state supporting his enemies on that state's home territory. The IRA, while operating mostly in Northern Ireland, has attacked the British in London, for example, and the Chechens have attacked the Russians in Moscow, both locales far from the territory being contested. Another specialty of Osama is the use of fanatical suicide bombers, though he has not been unique in that practice, which has been used by Palestinians in Israel, as well as by terrorists in India and Sri Lanka and elsewhere.

Which brings me briefly to the Israel-Palestine conflict. Osama is a latecomer to the Palestinian cause, and he added that to his objectives because he knows that it resonates well and widely in the Arab and Muslim worlds. And that conflict brings to mind another point. Governments of various kinds in various places fighting dissident and rebellious movements or groups have learned to label their opponents "terrorists," knowing that it is a term of opprobrium that cancels any legitimacy they might have, whereas these groups may simply be trying to liberate themselves from an oppressive and often foreign regime. Calling them "terrorists" is supposed to bring sympathetic support from other governments and people not involved in the conflict, for by definition a "terrorist" is an evil person who does not value human life at all, and is indiscriminate in choosing his targets. In popular opinion a suicide bomber is not only evil but also a fanatic, and thus somehow deranged, or less than human.

I don't think I need to cite examples, but a recent

89

one is the Russians labeling as "terrorists" the Chechens fighting for an independent Chechnya. It is almost amusing to hear the two sides now fighting over Afghanistan labeling each other "terrorists." So now everyone is a terrorist. If that is so, Kinsley is right that it is impossible to define "terrorism."

Before leaving this subject, I would like to make one final point, which will no doubt sound unpleasant to some listeners. Prime Minister Sharon has been quoted as saying that he cannot make peace with Yasser Arafat because Arafat is a terrorist, the chief terrorist on the Palestinian side. Well, Israel elects its leaders democratically, and for a country under siege it may not be surprising that three of its chosen leaders during the past half-century have been retired army generals. But what are we to conclude from the fact that two of Israel's leaders, two of its prime ministers, Yitzhak Shamir and Menachem Begin, are viewed by one side as former terrorists and by the other as freedom fighters?

I recently read a chronology of "Violence in the Holy Land" for the period March 1, 1947, to May 15, 1948, based on published material in *The Middle East Journal* at the time. It is a truly amazing compilation, cataloguing violence that was at least as bad as, if not worse than, what has been experienced recently. During one 40-day period (Nov. 30, 1947, to Jan. 10, 1948) 1,974 people were killed or injured. The killed included 295 Arabs, 262 Jews, and 30 British, an average of 15 people per day.

One of the most reprehensible acts of violence occurred after the period covered by that chronology. It occurred on September 17, 1948, well after the independence of Israel, so it could not be justified as part of the struggle by freedom fighters to create and establish a state for the Jewish people. It was the assassination of

Count Folke Bernadotte, the United Nations mediator for Palestine, the man assigned to bring peace to the area. There is no doubt that this act was carried out by extremists with a background of good terrorist credentials.

But the Middle East is not our best example. Nelson Mandela was sentenced to life imprisonment for terrorism. He spent 27 years in prison. He was repeatedly offered his freedom if he would order the African National Congress liberation movement to renounce violence. He refused, saying if the South African government would renounce violence against his people, he would reciprocate. He was eventually released and was elected president of South Africa. One man's terrorist is another man's ... what?

NELSON MANDELA:
HIS LONG WALK TO FREEDOM

South Africa is a very large subject indeed. It would clearly be impossible to give you even a once-over-lightly impression of this vast and complex country, its long history and highly developed economy, its myriad peoples and cultures, in a single lecture, which is my allotment as we travel along South Africa's southern and eastern coasts during the first five days of this segment of our "Silver Wind" cruise. With stops at six of its major port cities in this part of the country you will have ample exposure to the country's variety and beauty and the vibrant life of its people.

So I have elected to try to tell you the story of modern South Africa since World War II by examining the life of one man whose personal story during all of those years contains within it most of the principal issues and events of that history. The fact that I can do so is remarkable, and it is because that man is a remarkable person. I plan to tell you the story of Nelson Mandela, the current president of South Africa, in as factual a way as I can, based largely on his own autobiography, *Long Walk to Freedom*. (Published by Little, Brown and Company. Copyright © 1994 by Nelson Rolihlahla Mandela.)

Mandela was born on July 18, 1918, at Mvezo, a tiny village on the banks of the Mbashe River in the district of Umtata, the capital of Transkei. His middle

---

This lecture was delivered on November 28, 1997, on board Silversea Cruises' "Silver Wind" sailing off East London, South Africa.

name, "Rolihlahla," is his African name. In Xhosa, the language of the region, it literally means "pulling the branch of a tree," but its colloquial meaning is "troublemaker," which proves that someone, perhaps his father, was prescient. His more familiar English or Christian name was bestowed on him on his first day at school, by an English-educated teacher, of course, who was perhaps an admirer of Lord Nelson, the great English admiral. Perhaps he's lucky he wasn't also given the moniker "Horatio," Lord Nelson's first name.

Mandela was born into the Thembu tribe, part of the Xhosa nation. By both bloodline and custom his father was a chief. The larger ethnic group was known as the Nguni people, who include the Zulu and Swazi in the north, and the Xhosa in the south. So at his birth, and this has stayed with him throughout his life, Nelson Mandela was a child of the Madiba clan, the Thembu tribe, the Xhosa nation, and the Nguni people. These are all very important distinctions. In Africa, this is one's identity, never to be changed, or surrendered, or denied. For all of his life, and still today, despite all of the other things he is and has become, Mandela is called "Madiba" by his intimates, his relatives and close friends, the clan name with which he was born. I stress this because it tells you how far one man has come in one lifetime.

He was a member of a royal household, but was not in the line of succession to become the monarch of his people, the Thembu tribe. His father was known as a stubborn man, a trait Mandela thought he inherited. Although illiterate, the father played the role of historian of the Xhosa nation, in the oral tradition. He also greatly respected education, which served his son well. The father had four wives, and altogether 13 children. Nelson, a junior son of the third wife, was not destined to be a chief or for other high office. The father was rebellious as well as stubborn, and this caused him to defy a British magistrate, who deposed him as chief and took away his lands and cattle, thus his fortune. Nearly destitute, Nelson's mother moved with her son to the village of Qunu, where she would have the support of relatives and friends. Though raised in poverty, Nelson remembered the years of his boyhood in Qunu village as happy ones.

At the age of five he became a herd-boy, tending sheep and calves. At that early age he discovered the almost mystical attachment that the Xhosa people have to cattle, not only as a source of food and wealth but as a blessing from God and a source of happiness. His mother became a Christian and Nelson was baptized as a Methodist. This was his entrée to school, a one-room school. His father did not convert but approved of schooling, and gave him a pair of his own trousers, cut off at the knee so they would fit, as he wanted his son to be properly attired at school. Before that Nelson's only garment had been the traditional blanket worn by Xhosa people.

When Nelson was nine his father died, causing a major change in his life. His mother took him on a long journey by foot to the Great Place of the Thembu king, presided over by a regent, who became Nelson's guardian for the next decade. His school became another one-room affair, but much more modern, as it was part of a Methodist mission station attached to the chief's Great Place. Nelson's life was now governed by two poles: the chieftaincy and the church. His nickname now was "Grandpa" because he was a very serious lad and to his playmates looked like an old man.

When he was 16 the regent decided it was time that Nelson became a man. In Xhosa tradition that is achieved through one means only: circumcision. This ritual formally incorporates boys into society. In his book

Mandela describes in great detail how he and 25 other boys together passed through this elaborate ceremony, and as distant as a Westerner might feel from this nearly universal African custom, one has to appreciate its significance in creating the sense of community that is one of the strengths of tribally organized societies.

Now having taken this essential step, Nelson could marry, set up a home, plow his own field, and join the councils of the community, where he could speak and be taken seriously. He also acquired a new name, a circumcision name: Dalibunga, which means "founder of the Bungha," the traditional ruling body of the Transkei.

The regent, Nelson's guardian, decreed that unlike most of his companions who were destined to work in the white man's gold mines, Nelson was to become a counselor to the Thembu king, and for that he needed higher education. He was therefore sent to Clarkebury Boarding Institute. Before his departure, a sheep was slaughtered in his honor, there was dancing and singing, and he received from the regent his first pair of boots. The boarding school was at another Methodist mission in the Transkei, at the time the highest institution of learning for Africans in Thembuland. It was both a secondary school and a teacher training college.

In the first days at school he walked so awkwardly in the boots he was not used to wearing that he caused a couple of sophisticated girls to laugh at him. One girl whispered to the other: "The country boy's not used to wearing shoes." Nelson overheard and was mortified and embarrassed, but as that emotion wore off he became friends with one of the girls, Mathona by name. She was his first true female friend, his best friend at school, someone he could confide in and share secrets with. She was the model for all of his subsequent friendships with women, for with women he found he could let his hair down and confess to weaknesses and fears that he would never dare reveal to another man.

Nelson worked hard at that school, which was strict and demanding, and graduated in two years instead of three. He lost touch with Mathona, who was gifted and worthy of higher education, but her parents lacked the means. Nelson noted that this was an all too typical South African story; it was not lack of ability that held his people back, but lack of opportunity. At that time, when he was 19, his horizon did not extend beyond becoming a counselor to the Thembu king, but he moved on to Healdtown, the Methodist college in Fort Beaufort, a white town where Xhosas had once lived and farmed. The college drew students from all over the country, but they tended to segregate themselves along tribal lines when they could. Still, Nelson learned about the varieties of folk who made up the black people of South Africa, and made his first friends outside his own tribe.

In his final year at Healdtown he had his consciousness raised by the visit of a renowned Xhosa poet or praise-singer who instilled in him pride as an African but even more so as a Xhosa, and he began to sense that whites were not always benefactors but could also be oppressors. He moved on to the University College of Fort Hare at Alice, the only residential center of higher education for blacks in South Africa, founded by Scottish missionaries. It was also a beacon for African scholars from all over southern, central, and eastern Africa. For young black South Africans like Mandela it was Oxford and Cambridge, Harvard and Yale all rolled into one, as he put it. On this occasion the regent bought Nelson his first full suit of clothes. He was 21 years old.

A fellow student at Fort Hare was K. D. Matanzima, Nelson's nephew according to tribal hierarchy, although Nelson was younger and far less senior in the tribe. We shall hear more of him later on. At this stage he took Nelson under his wing, for he was already a third-year student. Matanzima counseled him to study law, but Nelson had his heart set on becoming a civil servant, the highest office a black South African could aspire to, as an interpreter or clerk in the Native Affairs Department. Mandela had his first taste of politics and the pleasure of winning a contest against authority when he led a rebellion of the freshmen against the seniors who were harassing them, a campaign that succeeded in displacing the seniors as heads of the dormitory house committee.

Mandela was active in athletics and in dramatics, taking advantage of the fact that he was the second tallest student at Fort Hare. In a play Nelson had the role of John Wilkes Booth, the assassin of Abraham Lincoln, who was played by his fellow actor who was a bit taller. On the soccer field he met Oliver Tambo, later to become his law partner and fellow revolutionary at the head of the African National Congress.

Mandela's career at Fort Hare ended prematurely, without his receiving the bachelor's degree he was so much counting on to restore his family's fortunes, because of a series of disastrous events that tell a lot about his character. During his second year, a year short of his degree, he was elected to the student council, the highest student organization, but refused to take his seat because his election grew out of a student boycott that he had supported. The principal, a dour Scot, insisted that he take the seat or else he would have to expel him from the college. Mandela stood on principle and refused to comply. The college head then told him to think it over during the holidays, after which he could return to Fort Hare only if he agreed to accept the position he had been elected to.

A very troubled Mandela returned home to his guardian's Great Place, only to learn that the regent had arranged marriages for him and for his childhood pal, the regent's son named Justice, with two local girls from prominent families. Neither young man wanted any part of an arranged marriage, but the regent had already paid the bride price, known as *lobola*, and said there was no turning back. "At that time," Mandela recalled, "I was more advanced socially than politically. While I would not have considered fighting the political system of the white man, I was quite prepared to rebel against a social system of my own people." Ironically, he blamed the regent for this attitude, which resulted from the advanced education that the regent had provided for him.

But the regent insisted on the arranged marriages. In desperation Mandela and his pal made a plan to run away to Johannesburg, first selling two of the regent's oxen without his permission to get the money to pay their way to the big city. The regent suspected what they were up to and nearly thwarted their scheme, but they succeeded in talking and bribing their way out of town, and eventually had to resort to hitchhiking with the mother of the employer of a friend, an elderly white woman who extracted a large fee for the favor.

They traveled without the documents required of all blacks leaving their home district, so it was a dangerous trip, but they reached the vast bright lights of Johannesburg, with no money, no prospects, no college degree, and fortunately, as they saw it, no wives. In those days for country boys of whatever station Jo'burg was, to quote Mandela's own description, the "city of dreams, a place where one could transform oneself from a poor peasant to a wealthy sophisticate, a city of danger and of opportunity ... [a city] of buildings so tall you could not see the tops, of crowds of people speaking languages you had never heard of, of sleek motorcars and beautiful women and dashing gangsters ... the city of gold." Mandela did not realize that this was not the end of a journey, but rather "the very beginning of a much longer and more trying journey that would test [him] in ways that [he] could not then have imagined." Except for when he was in hiding, or on the run from the police, or the many years spent in prison, Jo'burg would be his home for most of the rest of his life.

I have focused a lot of attention on Mandela's early years through his university days because that part of his story is less well-known than are his political activist and prison years and eventual triumph, and because those formative years tell us much that we need to know about how he was formed and what made him what he is today.

In Johannesburg the two young men found employment at the Crown Mines on the Rand, Justice as a clerk and Mandela as a lowly mine policeman and night watchman. This was his first opportunity to observe South African capitalism at close hand, and how the white owners and managers treated the black workers in this very dangerous trade of mining gold underground. A message from the regent caught up with them, telling the mine management to send the boys home to the Transkei immediately, and they were fired when they refused to comply. Looking for a job with the help of a cousin, Mandela had a fateful meeting with a real estate agent who specialized in housing for Africans, whose name was Walter Sisulu, a man who would change Mandela's life.

Sisulu, though minimally educated, was a successful businessman and community leader. Mandela told him that his ambition was to become a lawyer, and to finish his bachelor's degree by taking correspondence courses through the University of South Africa. Sisulu recommended him to a white Jewish lawyer named Lazar Sidelsky, a progressive man who was willing to take on an African as an articled clerk. Mandela soon fell under the spell of the law firm's only other African employee, Gaur Radebe, who was indeed a "troublemaker" as a member of both the African National Congress and the Communist Party. Mandela attended some meetings of the latter, as part of his new urban education.

But Mandela was far from prospering in Jo'burg. He was paid a pittance and lived in poverty as a boarder in Alexandra Township. Mr. Sidelsky, who was Mandela's height, gave him an old suit of his. Assisted by stitching and patching, Nelson wore that same suit for five years, so that in the end it was more patches than suit. He re-encountered Ellen Nkabinde, whom he had known slightly at Healdtown College. She was now a teacher in one of the township schools. They fell in love, but the romance faded, partly because Nelson's friends objected to the fact that Ellen was a Swazi rather than a Xhosa. It is true that the South African whites under the apartheid regime exploited the tribal divisions among the black populace, but it is also true that tribal loyalties and enmities often overwhelmed that black population and prevented them from cooperating more to further their own liberation from oppression.

The regent died suddenly in the winter of 1942. Mandela felt guilty over how he had treated his longtime guardian, but his shame was somewhat mitigated by the fact that he had met personally with the regent and reconciled with him before his death. At the funeral Mandela realized that his future was no longer bound up with Thembuland and the Transkei, and his aspirations now exceeded having a career in the civil service as an interpreter in the Native Affairs Department. Thus began a lifelong inner conflict, between his heart and his head, as Mandela put it, between his obligations to his family and tribe, and the calling he now felt to work on behalf of his entire people, that is, the liberation struggle of the black people of South Africa.

He returned to Jo'burg and passed his examinations for his bachelor's degree, and thus became a graduate of Fort Hare University. But education was not enough. His colleague Gaur Radebe convinced him that if the Africans relied on education for their liberation they would wait a thousand years for their freedom. The engine of change, he said, was the African National Congress, founded in 1912. Its constitution denounced racialism, its presidents had been from different tribal groups, and it preached the goal of Africans as full citizens of South Africa. Mandela's first participation in the struggle came in August 1943, when he joined a 10,000-man march in support of the Alexandra bus boycott protesting a one-pence fare increase that fell hardest on poor Africans. He found the experience exhilarating and inspiring, and was also impressed that the protest succeeded in rolling back the fare increase.

His boss Mr. Sidelsky warned him to stay away from politics if he wanted to be a successful lawyer, but Mandela was already recruited by politics. When Radebe left the firm to start his own real estate agency, Mandela, now the sole African employee of the firm, was articled as a clerk. And he now enrolled at the University of the Witwatersrand to work for a bachelor of laws degree, the ticket to becoming a lawyer. "Wits," as it is called, is the premier English-speaking university in South Africa. Mandela was the only African student in the law faculty.

He encountered much racial hostility from his fellow students, but also made lasting friendships with others, for example Joe Slovo and his future wife, Ruth First, children of Jewish immigrants and ardent

Communists; George Bizos, the child of Greek immigrants; and Bram Fischer, the scion of a distinguished Afrikaner family, as well as several Indian students from Natal. All became brave and staunch participants in the freedom struggle.

Mandela says there was no epiphany, no moment of revelation or truth, that politicized him. It was a steady accumulation of a thousand slights, a thousand indignities, that produced in him an anger, a rebelliousness, a desire to fight the system that imprisoned his people. It was the extreme segregation that meant "an African child is born in an Africans Only hospital, taken home on an Africans Only bus, lives in an Africans Only area, and attends Africans Only schools, if he attends school at all. When he grows up, he can hold Africans Only jobs, rent a house in Africans Only townships, ride Africans Only trains, and be stopped at any time of the day or night and be ordered to produce a pass, failing which he will be arrested and thrown in jail." Mandela simply found himself fighting for the liberation of his people because he could not do otherwise.

Walter Sisulu recruited him into the ANC, and he soon became one of the organizers of the ANC Youth League in 1944. It was designed to revitalize the somewhat moribund ANC, to mobilize mass support, recruit new members, and launch a campaign of action. Mandela points out that the crippling, discriminatory anti-African legislation greatly pre-dated the regime of "grand apartheid" instituted by the Afrikaner governments that came to power in 1948, going all the way back to the 1913 Land Act that ultimately deprived blacks of 87 percent of the territory in the land of their birth. Other laws of the '20s and '30s created the teeming African slums, barred Africans from practicing skilled trades, substituted the British Crown for the traditional paramount chiefs, and removed all Africans from the voters' roll in the Cape. He also says the Youth Leaguers were wary of Communism, and of all other foreign ideologies. One reason was that the Communist Party was dominated by whites. Early on Mandela opted for pure African nationalism over any competing ideology.

Mandela met his first wife, Evelyn, at Walter Sisulu's home. She was an orphan, a relative of the Sisulus whom they treated like a daughter, and she was in training to be a nurse. They fell in love and were married within a few months. Unable to afford a traditional wedding or feast, they were married in a civil ceremony. Their biggest problem was finding a place to live, and they had to resort to moving in first with Evelyn's brother and then with her sister.

The electoral victory of the Afrikaner National Party in 1948 made *de jure* what had previously been *de facto*: the entrenchment of white supremacy and the oppression of blacks, Coloureds, and Indians. Under new, more militant leadership, the ANC in response turned to mass mobilization. It mounted a Freedom Day strike and a Defiance Campaign, in which ANC people defied unjust laws and did not resist arrest. Going to prison became a badge of honor. Mandela was elected president of the Transvaal ANC, and in 1952 he became first deputy president of the ANC, under Zulu Chief Albert Luthuli as the new president. A new, more activist era for the ANC began at that time.

The government tried to get Luthuli to renounce his membership in the ANC, but the proud Zulu chief who was also a devout Christian refused to abandon his principles and was as a result deposed from his chieftaincy. In an attempt to stifle the ANC the government banned Mandela and 51 other ANC leaders for six months. These banning orders prevented those affected from attending any meeting of any kind or even of talking to more than one person at a time. Thus, Mandela was unable to attend his son's birthday party. Anticipating that the government would try to declare the ANC an illegal organization, the leaders encouraged Mandela to draw up a plan to enable the ANC to continue operating underground. This strategy became known as the Mandela Plan.

In the meantime Mandela, with a growing family, also had to earn his livelihood. An indifferent student of law at Wits, he abandoned his effort to obtain a law degree after failing his exams several times. But he did complete his articles and passed a qualifying exam so that he could begin to practice as an attorney. After brief stints at several white law firms (there were no black firms then) and being outraged that one of them charged poor African clients higher fees than they did their affluent white clients, in August 1952 Mandela opened his own law office in downtown Jo'burg, and soon took as his partner Oliver Tambo, a deeply religious man and formidable debater who had been Mandela's schoolmate at Fort Hare. The new and only all-African firm in town was besieged with clients from the beginning, and it soon became for Africans the firm of first choice and last resort.

In what he admitted was a somewhat rabble-rousing public speech, Mandela for the first time stated that he thought passive resistance had failed, and that non-violence could never overturn a ruthless white minority regime determined on retaining its power at any cost. He said his people had to be prepared to use the weapon of violence if necessary. This was not an impulsive statement, as Mandela had been analyzing the situation in South Africa and had concluded that the tactics used by Gandhi in India would not work for the

ANC because in the Indian case the protesters faced a British regime that was not prepared to go to the extreme measures to stamp out dissent that the Afrikaners then ruling South Africa were prepared to use. For departing from approved policy in this speech Mandela was reprimanded by his superiors in the ANC.

Soon Mandela, then 35 years old, received a much more severe banning order under the strangely named Suppression of Communism Act. He was required to resign from the ANC, was restricted to the Johannesburg district, and could not attend any meetings or gatherings for two years. The Law Society of the Transvaal also tried to disbar him for his political activities, but able lawyers, including some Afrikaners, came to his defense, using the argument that leading members of the National Party, including future Prime Minister B. J. Vorster, had been detained for expressing pro-Nazi political views during the Second World War, but had not been disbarred for that reason. Mandela prevailed.

In June 1955 the ANC held a Congress of the People. More than 3,000 delegates braved police intimidation to assemble and approve a Freedom Charter that in essence demanded the establishment of democracy in South Africa and equal rights for all races. Most delegates were blacks, but there were more than 300 Indians, 200 Coloureds, and 100 whites. Later that year Mandela's banning order expired. He visited his home territory and bought a small plot of land in Umtata, the capital. He also tried to persuade his cousin and former mentor, K. D. Matanzima, whom he called by his tribal name--Daliwonga--now the chief of their tribe, to join the struggle. The latter refused, determined to assert his traditional royal prerogatives, and in fact he succeeded, for he eventually became the leader of the Transkei homeland or Bantustan, a collaborator with the apartheid regime. Mandela regretted that at that point they were leading entirely antagonistic camps among the African people of the country.

The next year Mandela was banned for the third time, for five years on this occasion, and in December 1956 he was arrested, jailed, and charged with "high treason." He was only one of 156 people arrested as the government made a nationwide sweep of the leadership of the liberation struggle. This number included 105 Africans, 21 Indians, 23 whites, and 7 Coloureds. The action was a deliberate effort by the regime to decapitate the ANC and other protesting organizations. At a hearing to determine if they were to be tried in the Supreme Court, the prisoners were herded into a large wire cage that had been constructed in the courtroom. This not only kept them from communicating with their lawyers, but had a symbolic value as well. One prisoner scribbled a sign on a piece of paper and posted it on the side of the cage. It read: "Dangerous. Please Do Not Feed."

The prisoners were released on bail, pending trial. Mandela's marriage had been deteriorating for some time, and the final break came when he found on being released from jail that Evelyn had left their home with their children and had moved in with her brother. Their irreconcilable differences arose over religion and politics. Evelyn had converted to the faith of the Jehovah's Witnesses and tried to convert her husband. He objected strongly to what he regarded as her faith's passivity in the face of oppression, and she objected just as strongly to his devotion to the liberation struggle, which was now consuming most of his time and energy.

At the preparatory trial the prosecution's presentation lasted for 10 months, including 8,000 pages of typed evidence and 12,000 documents. Three months later charges against 61 of the accused, including Chief

Luthuli and Oliver Tambo, were dropped. While awaiting trial in the Supreme Court, Mandela met his future wife Winnie, who had called on his partner Oliver Tambo on a legal matter. Having completed her studies, she was working as the first black social worker at the premier black hospital in Jo'burg, Baragwanath Hospital. Her given name was "Nomzamo," which means one who strives or undergoes trials, a name as prophetic as Nelson's tribal name of "Rolihlahla." She came from Pondoland, an area adjacent to the part of Transkei where Nelson had grown up. Her great-grandfather had been a powerful chief in Natal. They were married in June 1958.

Before the trial scheduled to begin in August 1958, the government withdrew its indictment and issued a new one, charging only 30 of the accused, all members of the ANC, including Mandela. The actual trial began a full year later. In March 1960, as Chief Luthuli was testifying for the defense, a major event brought world attention to the struggle in South Africa. The recently formed Pan Africanist Congress, a militant African nationalist organization that rejected the multiracialism of the ANC and was led by Robert Sobukwe, launched an anti-pass defiance campaign in competition with the ANC, the leaders inviting arrest. Sobukwe was arrested and sentenced to three years' imprisonment. Demonstrations in support of those arrested erupted, and a large one at Sharpeville, a small township south of Jo'burg, became world news when panicky police fired on unarmed protesters, killing 69 of them and wounding over 400. Sharpeville was labeled a massacre and provoked a government crisis. There was outrage across the globe and the UN Security Council intervened in South African affairs for the first time. The Jo'burg stock exchange plunged, capital began to flee the country, and some whites made plans to emigrate. But the government refused to make any concessions toward racial equality, insisted that Sharpeville was a Communist conspiracy, and imposed martial law.

Mandela and his colleagues were now rearrested under the new State of Emergency. More than 2,000 were detained in a nationwide sweep. Both the ANC and the PAC were declared illegal, and membership in them made a felony with imprisonment for up to 10 years. Oliver Tambo left the country to strengthen the ANC abroad now that it had been suppressed at home. When the trial resumed the defense lawyers withdrew in protest, and each defendant now conducted his own defense, a tactic designed to drag the trial out even longer. In his own statement Mandela stressed the ANC's commitment to non-violence.

Months later the Emergency was lifted and the prisoners released, but the trial continued for another nine months until March 1961. While awaiting the verdict, the ANC decided that if he was acquitted Mandela would go underground. After a trial that had lasted four years, the three-judge panel surprisingly acquitted all of the defendants, and said the ANC had not tried to overthrow the state by violence, and was not a Communist organization. The state was embarrassed and was determined that there would be no repetition of this humiliation.

Mandela did not return home after the verdict but spent the night in a safe house and then went underground, leaving Jo'burg behind. He toured the country, meeting secretly with ANC cadres. He tried to make himself invisible. He stopped shaving and cutting his hair. He wore overalls and disguised himself as a chauffeur, a chef, or a "garden boy." The best disguise was as a chauffeur, for it permitted him to travel by car, pretending to be his master's driver. He acquired the legendary nickname of "The Black Pimpernel."

Some of the ANC leadership despaired that non-violence could succeed. Mandela was thus authorized to establish a military organization separate from the ANC. Mandela was a military novice, and he realized that he and his organization were now embarking on a new and dangerous course, one of organized violence, the results of which could not be known. The aim was to begin with what was least violent to individuals but most damaging to the state. Given its fledgling nature, sabotage was the only available tactic at the beginning. The name of the new organization would be "The Spear of the Nation." The symbol of the spear was chosen because with this simple weapon Africans had resisted the incursions of whites for centuries.

From underground Mandela sent a letter to the newspapers in which he confirmed that the police were seeking to arrest him. He said he had chosen to live as an outlaw, in poverty, separated from his family. He would not surrender, he would not leave South Africa, and he would "continue fighting for freedom until the end of [his] days." His hideout became an ANC-owned farm in Rivonia, a bucolic northern suburb of Jo'burg, where he pretended to be a houseboy or caretaker using the alias David Motsamayi. Winnie and the children occasionally visited him on weekends, taking extreme precautions to avoid surveillance.

Afrikaners were stunned when Chief Luthuli was awarded the Nobel Peace Prize. By coincidence Mandela had chosen the same time frame to announce the formation of The Spear of the Nation and its manifesto, selecting as the date December 16, the day South African whites celebrate their defeat of the great Zulu leader Dingane at the Battle of Blood River in 1838. Afrikaners celebrate that date as the triumph of their tribe over the black Africans and the demonstration that God was on their side. That December 16, the day after Chief Luthuli returned from Oslo with his prize, the Spear announced its presence by setting off explosions of homemade bombs at electric power stations and government offices in Jo'burg, Port Elizabeth, and Durban.

Mandela traveled abroad to represent the ANC at conferences, and visited Tanzania, Ethiopia, Egypt, Tunisia, Morocco, Ghana, Mali, Guinea, Sierra Leone, Liberia, Senegal, and the Sudan. He was impressed to see so many countries now ruled by black Africans, as many of these countries had won their independence in the early 1960s. He returned to South Africa and while driving from Durban to Jo'burg, wearing his chauffeur's disguise, he was arrested by the police and imprisoned in Jo'burg. The ANC mounted "Free Mandela" demonstrations, and to thwart them the government moved the preliminary hearing to Pretoria. Mandela wore traditional Xhosa garb--a leopard-skin kaross--in the courtroom, to show his defiance. His intention was to put the state on trial.

This time there was no possibility of denying that he had been working to overthrow the regime by force, but he challenged the court by saying he was not morally bound to obey laws made by a parliament in which he had no representation. He called no witnesses and rested his case. Coincident with the end of the trial the United Nations voted for sanctions against South Africa for the first time. Mandela made an eloquent statement when given a chance to address the court in a plea in mitigation, an hour-long political statement in which he argued that he had been driven to become an outlaw by the persecution of his people. Despite knowing the dreadful conditions suffered by Africans imprisoned in his country, he assured the court that imprisonment would not sway him, and that when he emerged after completing his sentence he would "take up again, as best I can, the struggle for the removal of those injustices until they are finally abolished once and for all." After a 10-minute recess the magistrate pronounced the sentence: five years with no possibility of parole, the stiffest sentence yet imposed for a political offense.

In prison Mandela refused to wear the shorts given to all African prisoners in keeping with the attitude that all African men were "boys," and he refused to eat the pitiful food provided to Africans. The head warder compromised with him and agreed he could wear long trousers and have his own food if he would agree to be put in solitary confinement. For a while Mandela accepted this deal.

The authorities were not yet through with Mandela. He was transferred to the notorious Robben Island prison offshore from Cape Town, South Africa's Alcatraz, where conditions were incredibly harsh, and the guards notorious for their brutality. Nine months into his sentence Mandela learned that the authorities had raided the ANC farm in Rivonia, had confiscated hundreds of documents, and had then arrested the entire leadership of Spear of the Nation. The subsequent trial, known as the Rivonia Trial, was one of the most significant in South Africa's history. The accused were charged with over 200 acts of sabotage and conspiracy to overthrow the government, the penalty for which was death by hanging. Mandela was moved to Pretoria from Robben Island to enter the dock with the other accused.

Mandela spent a fortnight drafting his statement to the court, and declined the advice of his attorneys to moderate it lest he provoke the authorities into handing down the harshest possible sentence. He spoke first for the defense, as accused number one, who admittedly had organized Spear of the Nation. This eloquent statement, which lasted four hours, was subsequently published and confirmed Nelson Mandela ever afterward as the leader of the struggle against apartheid. It was printed word for word in South Africa's *Rand Daily Mail* newspaper, despite the fact that all of Mandela's words were banned. Not having time to quote extensively from it, including his remarks expressing great admiration for the examples of the British and American democracies, I will read you the final paragraph only, which he spoke from memory while looking directly at the presiding judge, in a courtroom that had suddenly become extremely quiet:

> During my lifetime I have dedicated myself to this struggle of the African people. I have fought against white domination, and I have fought against black domination. I have cherished the ideal of a democratic and free society in which all persons live together in harmony and with equal opportunities. It is an ideal which I hope to live for and to achieve. But if needs be, it is an ideal for which I am prepared to die.

On June 12, 1964, all of the principal accused were convicted and sentenced to life imprisonment. Though the government denied it, international pressure had prevented sentences of death from being imposed. Nelson Mandela, then 46 years old, and his closest associates spent the next 25 years in prison, 18 of those years on Robben Island, until Mandela and a few others were transferred, in 1982, to Pollsmoor Maximum Security Prison on the mainland a few miles southeast of Cape Town. Mandela called Pollsmoor a five-star hotel compared with Robben Island.

Robben Island prisoners were allowed to send one letter no longer than 500 words to their families every six months. Winnie Mandela was banned, then fired from her job as a social worker, and later arrested, brutally interrogated, and jailed for 17 months. Mandela's mother died, but he was not allowed to attend the funeral. His son was killed in an auto accident, and again he was not allowed to attend the funeral. Later on his and Winnie's house in Orlando West was destroyed by arsonists. For 13 years the prisoners worked a lime quarry, make-work of the most degrading sort. Newspapers were contraband. Warders tried to trick Mandela into trying to escape so that they could kill him.

About a particularly brutal warder Mandela wrote: "He was not evil; his inhumanity had been foisted upon him by an inhuman system. He behaved like a brute because he was rewarded for brutish behavior." Mandela wrote a draft of his memoirs in prison, but when the manuscript was accidentally discovered all prisoners lost their study privileges for four years. Mandela was offered a chance to leave prison and live in the Transkei if he would recognize the legitimacy of that Bantustan, now ruled by his cousin Matanzima. He declined the offer. Winnie was exiled to the town of Brandfort. Through it all Mandela was convinced he would survive and would emerge from prison a free man.

I wish I had time to tell you the full story of Mandela's life in prison, but I do not have sufficient time left, and that part of his life is much better known because from then on he became the focus of the liberation struggle in South Africa. Even though a prisoner, or because he was perhaps the most famous political prisoner, he was recognized around the world as the man with whom the regime would have to deal and compromise if the bloodshed was to be ended in South Africa and a government that recognized the equal rights of all South Africans could come to power.

Late in his incarceration Mandela was visited by South African and foreign envoys who offered him his freedom if he would renounce violence. This offer was made public by Prime Minister P.W. Botha. Mandela's answer was that it was up to the South African government to renounce the violence it was using against the African population. His response was made public by his daughter. Mandela challenged Botha to renounce violence, and apartheid, and to unban the ANC.

Following a prostate operation in 1985 Mandela began to receive approaches from South African officials about possible negotiations. These contacts were sporadic and Mandela held out for his basic principles with no compromise. The only major change was an improvement in his prison conditions. In 1988 he was given a three-room suite in the prison where he could work, rather than an isolated cell. Later he was moved to a cottage on the grounds of the Victor Verster prison, a sort of halfway house between prison and freedom. His life had now become luxurious compared with Robben Island. His warder, Mr. Swart, was a friendly Afrikaner and skilled cook who prepared excellent meals for him.

Mandela had a personal meeting with P.W. Botha, who later had a stroke and resigned as president in August 1989. F.W. de Klerk replaced him and affirmed his commitment to reform. He began releasing the ANC prisoners and announced that the "time for negotiations has arrived." Mandela was finally released on February 11, 1990, after 27 and a half years in prison. He was 71 years old. President Bush was the first world leader to telephone Mandela after his release to offer his congratulations. The ANC renounced violence, and talks with the South African government became serious. Oliver Tambo, Mandela's closest friend and law partner, died of a stroke just as agreement was reached for the first democratic elections in South Africa. Mandela and de Klerk were awarded the 1993 Nobel Peace Prize, as Bishop Desmond Tutu had been in 1984. On April 27, 1994, Mandela exercised the franchise for the first time and voted for the ANC, which received 62.6 percent of the vote. On May 10 he was inaugurated as president of the first democratic, nonracial government of South Africa.

Reflecting on his life, Mandela wrote that he had "learned that courage was not the absence of fear, but the triumph over it. I felt fear myself more times than I can remember, but I hid it behind a mask of boldness. The brave man is not he who does not feel afraid, but he who conquers that fear." Looking back, he wrote that he never regretted the decision he had made as a young man when he joined the ANC and made his commitment to the struggle, and he was always prepared to face the hardships that affected him personally. "But," he wrote, "my family paid a terrible price, perhaps too dear a price for my commitment." That is the human dimension of the Mandela story.

Here are the next-to-last paragraphs of Mandela's autobiography:

It was during those long and lonely years that my hunger for the freedom of my own people became a hunger for the freedom of all people, white and black. I knew as well as I knew anything that the oppressor must be liberated just as surely as the oppressed. A man who takes away another man's freedom is a prisoner of hatred, he is locked behind the bars of prejudice and narrow-mindedness. I am not truly free if I am taking away someone else's freedom, just as surely as I am not free when my freedom is taken from me. The oppressed and the oppressor alike are robbed of their humanity.

When I walked out of prison, that was my mission, to liberate the oppressed and the oppressor both. Some say that has now been achieved. But I know that that is not the case. The truth is that we are not yet free; we have merely achieved the freedom to be free, the right not to be oppressed. We have not taken the final step of our journey, but the first step on a longer and even more difficult road. For to be free is not merely to cast off one's chains, but to live in a way that respects and enhances the freedom of others. The true test of our devotion to freedom is just beginning.

Publications of the
Five and Ten Press Inc.

This is a small, independent press that publishes high-quality (in content, if possible in presentation) paperback original works of fiction, nonfiction, and our specialty "factual fiction," in a variety of genres: memoirs, essays, short stories, novellas, miscellanies, and on one occasion poetry. All are published in limited first editions of from 400 to 600 copies, in 5" by 8" format that makes them convenient to carry in a coat pocket or purse while traveling on one conveyance or another. They rarely exceed 100 pages in length, so are not heavy to read in bed. The print font is fairly large, easy on the eyes.

They are always priced at between $5 and $10, hence the name of the press. They are sold individually from our web site (www.fiveandtenpress.com), by Internet booksellers such as amazon.com and barnesandnoble.com, and most successfully by subscription. Subscribers, of whom there are now more than 210, pay the press $25 in advance and receive, sight unseen, the next three or four publications. There are never any annoying charges for "shipping and handling," which for other presses are disguised profit centers. We mail by first-class postage, which guarantees delivery.

Despite our stringent editorial quality control, with the present volume we have thus far been able to publish 17 booklets. Many have been authored by Robert V. Keeley, but we have also published six other writers. The main criterion for publication is that the manuscript must show some wit, if possible a lot of wit. And secondly originality. Also, needless to say, readable style (not just "style"). Essentially we publish what mainstream (that is, commercial) publishers, magazines, newspapers, journals, and other outlets have no interest in and usually don't bother to respond to efforts to interest them in.

If you would like to subscribe, just send us a check for $25 and make sure you enclose your mailing address.

Five and Ten Press, Inc.
3814 Livingston Street N.W.
Washington, DC 20015-2803

If you would like to buy individual copies, here is our list, with prices shown. There are no discounts, and no charges for postage. New subscribers receive a free "signing bonus" copy of their choice of any of these titles.

By Robert V. Keeley:

1. D.C. Governance: It's Always Been a Matter of Race and Money. 29 pages. Published in December 1995, second printing in February 1996. (Out of print. Available in photocopy for $5.)

A brief history of home rule in the District of Columbia from its founding in 1800 through the end of self-governance in the 1870s, based on my grandfather's book written in 1916 entitled *Democracy or Despotism in the American Capital*. Part II examines the situation of the nation's capital today, arguing that it is ungovernable for basic structural reasons embedded in the Constitution and in the acts of Congress controlling its governance, and because of its unique characteristics that most critics ignore. Eight possible solutions are then briefly analyzed, with a conclusion that territorial status is the only viable solution.

2. Annals of Investing: Steve Forbes vs. Warren Buffett. 49 pages. March 1996. Second printing 2000. $5.

Part I, entitled "Steve Forbes for President? Not if You Want to Make Money in the Stock Market," begins with a highly negative critique of Forbes's flat tax proposal featured in his campaign for the 1996 Republican presidential nomination, and then recounts my black humor experience using the stock tips provided by the Forbes Special Situation Survey, an element of Forbes's publishing empire, to try to make money in the stock market, with devastatingly negative results.

Part II, entitled "Warren Buffett for President: What We Need in the White House Is a Real Eccentric," recounts the very positive results achieved by investing in Berkshire Hathaway, the investment vehicle of Warren Buffett of Omaha, Nebraska, the greatest American investor of modern times and a recognized genius.

An Appendix recounts in grimly humorous detail the actual results, mostly terrible, of using the Forbes Survey's stock tips to invest in 36 common stocks it recommended.

3. The File: A Princeton Memoir. 96 pages. May 1996. $10.

A frankly nostalgic, anecdotal account of my undergraduate years (1947-1951) at Princeton University. The anecdotes range over collegiate pranks, reform efforts, campus politics, undergraduate journalistic efforts, non-curricular escapades, disciplinary conflicts with the dean of the college, professorial mentors, imitations of F. Scott Fitzgerald, somewhat jejune literary endeavors, academic failures and near triumphs, and love affairs discreetly described. Most of this story is true, all of it is as remembered, and some is documented.

4. Essays Fast and Loose: A Christmas Miscellany. 76 pages. November 1996. $7.

Quirky essays about the O.J. Simpson trial, corporate executive greed, my sciatica and how Medicare prevents medical provider rip-offs, earning free cruises by dancing with unattached ladies, boredom induced by the Olympic Games, Colin Powell's deficiencies as a potential presidential candidate, and a wonderful Greek island.

5. Letters Mostly Unpublished. 72 pages. March 1997. $5.

Twenty-two letters to the editor and other unresponsive recipients about economics, presidential politics, parking tickets, recycling, Macedonia, the stock market, the State Department, Cambodia, ethnic cleansing, same-sex unions, Michael Eisner, Jack Valenti, Hiroshima, the Internet, the Internal Revenue Service, Newt Gingrich, and a lot of other targets.

6. Essays Cold and Hot: A New Year's Potpourri. 95 pages. January 1998. $10.

Another batch of original essays including a review of the condition of the District of Columbia as it approached its bicentennial celebration, analyses of two Supreme Court decisions that destroyed our Nationality Act and that precluded serious campaign finance reform, a reminiscence about the late controversial Prime Minister Andreas Papandreou of Greece, an argument that the U.S. Senate is behaving unconstitutionally, and a fantasy about Hollywood.

7. MSS Revisited. 72 pages. April 1998. $7.

A brief history of *MSS* magazine, an undergraduate literary journal published at Princeton University in 1949-51, followed by four *MSS* short stories authored by Jose Donoso, Walter Clemons, Jr., and R. V. Keeley. The stories concern a woman's nose job, a child's fear of his father, boredom at a gas company, and the Greek civil war. Included are obituaries of Donoso, the premier novelist of modern Chile, and of Clemons, a literary critic long featured in *Newsweek* magazine.

8. Three Sea Stories. 102 pages. Oct. 1999. $10.

Fictionalized memoirs. Lessons learned by a fairly innocent 16-year-old working as an engine room "wiper" on a merchant marine voyage, by an ambitious 24-year-old green ensign on U.S. Coast Guard weather patrol in the North Atlantic, and by a naive 29-year-old in a curious encounter with a hospitalized sea captain.

9. The Great Phelsuma Caper (A Diplomatic Memoir). 140 pages. December 2000. $10.

More "factual fiction." Phelsumas are day geckos, friendly small lizards that are harmless to humans but devastating to insects. They figure in the story, along with some pet birds (including toilet training one) and a few endangered species, and a notorious smuggling operation. But many human actors also appear, notably in some macabre adventures with Idi Amin Dada of Uganda. Cameo appearances are made by Richard Nixon, Queen Elizabeth II, Henry Kissinger, several U.S. senators, renowned criminal defense attorney Plato Cacheris, an eccentric avian ethologist, a Mauritian forester-bureaucrat, and several varieties of ambassadors. Locales include Uganda, Cambodia, Mauritius, Diego Garcia, Boston, San Antonio, and Washington. Most of the story is believable, but some of it, though true, is unbelievable.

10. Essays Near and Far: As a New Century Dawns. 116 pages. March 2002. $10.

By other authors:

11. Innocents of the Latter Day: Modern Americans Abroad. 98 pages. May 1997. $10. By Ambassador James W. Spain, a retired American Foreign Service officer, resident of Sri Lanka, and writer of distinction.

Eleven short stories about the Foreign Service of the United States, set in Pakistan, India, Bangladesh, Iran, Turkey, Greece, Kenya, Tanzania, and Switzerland. They tell of the ups and downs, ins and outs, problems and passions of the American diplomatic service, using wit, insight, satire, irony, and nostalgia to beguile the reader. They concern exasperating VIP visits, egomaniacal officials, missionaries with a mission, American exiles and lost souls, consular predicaments, spooky encounters, generation gaps, obnoxious host governments, and eccentric ambassadors.

12. Creatures of the Earth and the Mind. 60 pages. October 1998. $6. By Ambassador Carl Coon, a retired American Foreign Service officer, resident of Washington, D.C., and writer of distinction.

Ten charming and poignant essays and fictional stories mostly about animal life, starting with an encounter with Lord Ganesh the elephant god, moving on to a duck, a beaver, turkeys and vultures, 17-year locusts, and various pet dogs and cats, and ending with a provocative essay in which the author argues that the latest stage in the theory of biological evolutionary development concerns the "memes" of the human mind.

13. My Commute. 76 pages. December 1998. $14. ($10 for subscribers.) By Alison Autobound Axel.

This novella is a fictionalized memoir dedicated to

the disappeared of American corporate life. Its main motif, as the title suggests, is narrator Alison's commute to and from CHN Crumbles, Inc., a multinational corporation in which she works at a relatively low-level clerical job, in a cubicle. Alison has a vision, appropriate for the millennium, showing that for all of us to survive, workers must unite in a cooperative union, emulating the bees.

Alison's daily commute becomes a metaphor for her life as she interacts with the menaces on the highway and the equally grim hazards of company politics. Chinese fortune-cookie aphorisms become her guiding philosophy. Among the other characters are Freddie, a womanizing, vindictive manager; Stephanie, a young, fast-track executive who caters to Freddie and is mentored by him; Inez, another middle-management striver who tries to emulate him; Rose-Says-Not-to-Tell, a co-worker who relays company gossip; Celeste, a white-magic witch who tries to improve life in the department; and Janice, Alison's friend, who takes no nonsense from the corporate brass.

Alison's observations of her company's de-jobbing practices, its managers' strategies and foibles, and her co-workers' concerns, complaints, and day-to-day struggles to survive should hit home with any reader who has recently worked for a major American corporation.

14. Sic Transit. 68 pages. December 1999. $6. By Carl Coon, author of publication No. 12.

Another collection of essays, 13 this time, but of a quite different character. Some are satirical, some are humorous, all address the human condition by a writer who has a distinctive voice, is often eccentric, not always serious, possibly a curmudgeon, who admits at times to being an "old fogey." The subjects are power, the military mind, foreign affairs, Morocco, Nepal, marital relations, gender differences, generational differences, New York City, the pope, cyberspace, and lots more.

15. Poetry Mostly Off the Beaten Track. 56 pages. May 2001. $5. By Roy Herbert.

A course in understanding poetry, citing great poems of the past. Includes some previously unpublished poems by the late author, plus memorials by his widow and the publisher.

16. The Port of Missing Men (A Novel). 253 pages. June 2001. $10. By Alain Prévost. Translated from the French by Ralph Woodward, the author's Princeton roommate.

Grégoire, a French student at Princeton University, matures and learns sophistication through interactions with his American fellow undergraduates and via an affair with his widowed Aunt Laura. The late Alain Prévost was well-known in France for his fiction and nonfiction. None of his mature work has previously been translated into English.

17. Parting the Curtain: An American Teacher in Postcommunist Romania. 108 pages. August 2001. $10. By Anne Coe Heyniger.

"A remarkable series of carefully drawn pictures of life in that challenging country. Anne has the gift of almost photographic insight and economy of words. The stories are vivid and poignant; collectively they paint an impressive mural of political, economic, social and cultural change in an isolated but vibrant place. It is an elegantly written work, a true picture of time and place by a talented writer and sensitive observer."

Review by Frederick Quinn